ABOUT THE EDITORS

Noel Ward is a primary teacher in Tallaght who has had numerous articles published in educational journals. A former member of the Executive Committee of the Irish National Teachers' Organisation, he worked as a Programme Manager with the "Rainbow" Government of 1994 to 1997.

Triona Dooney is an Assistant Secretary with the Higher Education Authority. She was a contemporary of Michael Enright at University College Galway and a long-time political colleague. She was, like Michael, a founder member of Democratic Left and served with him on its National Executive.

Michael Enright Commemorative Project

IRISH EDUCATION FOR THE 21ST CENTURY

Edited by
Noel Ward
Triona Dooney

Oak Tree Press
Dublin

Oak Tree Press
Merrion Building
Lower Merrion Street
Dublin 2, Ireland
www.oaktreepress.com

A catalogue record of this book is
available from the British Library.

ISBN 1-86076-150-X

Printed in Ireland
by Colour Books Ltd, Dublin

Contents

ABOUT THE CONTRIBUTORS

Philomena Donnelly, a former primary teacher in Sutton, Co. Dublin, is a lecturer in St. Patrick's College of Education, Drumcondra.

Joe O'Toole is General Secretary of the Irish National Teachers' Organisation (INTO), an independent Senator, and Vice-President of the Irish Congress of Trade Unions (ICTU).

Richard Bruton, TD, is Fine Gael Spokesperson on Education and Science. He was Minister for Enterprise and Employment between 1994 and 1997.

Áine Hyland is Professor of Education and Vice-President at University College, Cork. Her published work includes three volumes of *Irish Educational Documents* of which she was co-editor.

Eamon Gilmore, TD, a former Minister at the Department of the Marine and Democratic Left Spokesperson on Education, is now Labour Party Spokesperson on the Environment.

Charles Lennon is General Secretary of the Association of Secondary Teachers in Ireland (ASTI).

Louis O'Flaherty is a former President of ASTI and author of *Management and Control in Irish Education: the Post-Primary Experience*.

Tony Deffely, a guidance counsellor in Castlebar, Co. Mayo, is a former President of the Teachers' Union of Ireland (TUI) and a member of the Minister for Education and Science Points Commission.

Jim Dorney is General Secretary of the Teachers' Union of Ireland (TUI).

Gearóid Ó Brádaigh is Chief Executive Officer of the Co. Westmeath Vocational Education Committee (VEC).

Brian Trench is a journalist and a lecturer in the School of Communications, Dublin City University. He is a member of the Irish Council for Science Technology and Innovation. In the late 1970s, he was, with Michael Enright, a member of the executive of the Socialist Labour Party.

Patrick Clancy is Professor at the Department of Social Science and the Social Science Research Centre, University College, Dublin. He is the author of a definitive series of studies on access to higher education in Ireland.

Séamus Puirséil is Director of the National Council for Educational Awards (NCEA) and a former President of the INTO.

Daniel O'Hare retired in August, 1999, as President of Dublin City University.

Kevin Hurley is Director of the Adult Education Programme at University College Dublin.

Peter Cassells is General Secretary of the Irish Congress of Trade Unions (ICTU).

Proinsias Ó Drisceoil is Arts Education Officer with Co. Kilkenny VEC and is widely published as a literary critic. He is a former teaching colleague of Michael Enright.

Edward Riordan lectures at the Cork Institute of Technology. He is a former President of the TUI and Chair of the National Centre for Guidance in Education.

Jim Cooke is a teacher at Ringsend Technical Institute, Dublin, and is at present compiling a history of the City of Dublin VEC.

Richard Langford is Chief Executive Officer of Cork City VEC. He was the Chairperson of TEASTAS, the interim National Certification Authority, on which Michael Enright served.

Micheál Martin, TD, has been Minister for Education and Science since June, 1997.

Foreword

This book came into existence as a means for colleagues in the worlds of politics and education to pay tribute to Michael Enright.

Michael was a family man, a teacher, a person of ideas and principle. He was a Democratic Left public representative in Wexford and a former Senator. He was also an active trade unionist, both through the Teachers' Union of Ireland and the Wexford Trades Council. His tragic death in a car crash in October 1997, at the age of 45, left his family and friends heartbroken and deprived his community of a distinguished and committed champion of social justice.

Michael's passion for politics and for education fused in his belief that education could and should be a powerful liberating force and a means towards a better life for the disadvantaged people on whose behalf he waged such effective battle. It was natural, therefore, that the unifying theme of this book of essays in his honour should be the future of education as we cross the threshold of the new century.

Colleagues across the political spectrum readily agreed to join Proinsias de Rossa, TD, MEP, and Alice Prendergast (President of Michael's union, the Teachers' Union of Ireland, 1996–1998), as sponsors of this project, in eloquent testimony to the respect and personal liking which Michael inspired. Our thanks go to Hugh Byrne, TD (Minister of State), Senator Brian Mullooly (Cathaoirleach, Seanad Éireann) of Fianna Fáil; Senator Avril Doyle, MEP, and Ivan Yates, TD, of Fine Gael; Brendan Howlin, TD, and Michael's colleague, Councillor Davy Hynes of the Labour Party.

Above all, we are grateful to the contributors to this book. Some of them knew Michael personally; others knew him only by reputation. But they all share his conviction that education can be a powerful agent for progressive change and they have given generously of their time and expertise to make this book a reality.

Our thanks are due also to David Givens of Oak Tree Press, who readily agreed to publish this book, and to Jenna Dowds who guided it through to publication. We would also like to thank Alice Prendergast, the TUI Executive, Kathy Flanagan and John Gallagher for their help with the project.

Finally, we wish to dedicate this book to Mary, Keira and Karla.

Triona Dooney
Noel Ward

September, 1999

Introduction

The pace of change and development in the field of education has rarely been faster. The last third of the twentieth century has witnessed significantly increased enrolment and investment, the development of new types of school and college and a legislative underpinning of the whole education system. There has also been, and continues to be, a good deal of reflection on the contribution of education to personal, economic and social development.

This book contributes to the ongoing discussion about the state of Irish education on the threshold of a new century and the various contributors examine issues which will be priorities for education planners in the early years of that century.

From Philomena Donnelly's reflections on how society treats young children — and especially those like Alice who live in poverty — to Daniel O'Hare's challenging improvement agenda for our universities, the writers range far and wide in their concerns. Joe O'Toole believes the coinciding interests of disparate groups will lead to significant changes in early childhood and primary education while Richard Langford suggests that different models of education in Europe are learning from one another to the benefit of the post-second-level sector. Investment in early school leavers and under-achievers are among the priorities identified by Áine Hyland; Tony Deffely argues that the system itself tempts some to leave early.

The debate on quality is emphasised in Richard Bruton's article, while Charles Lennon reflects on the high standing of our teachers and advocates consensus on issues of school evaluation. Gearóid Ó Bradaigh argues that management theory in education, as elsewhere, must take into account unpredictability factors and suggests that change will need careful, even protracted, preparation. Séamus Puirséil reviews developments and challenges at third-level, and Patrick Clancy shows that inequality stubbornly persists within this sector. With such issues in mind, Jim Dorney advocates the continued development of the further education sector, with suitable structures, accreditation and status.

Higher technological education's growth is traced by Ed Riordan who is optimistic about the future of an intellectually self-confident Institute of Technology sector. The Catholic Church's securing of a strong position in second-level school management is chronicled by Louis O'Flaherty who asks whether this can be maintained in a more secular society. Assumptions about the value of computers in schools are critically examined by Brian Trench, while Proinsias Ó Drisceoil queries whether, in the view of Southern-based organisations which are vocal about the position of Irish in schools, Protestant, and especially Northern Protestant, perspectives are "still alien there".

Three articles reflect on the state and future of lifelong learning as a process of forming public policy on adult education. Jim Cooke traces the unique contribution of the City of Dublin VEC in this sector and suggests that a system developed in adversity should be confirmed and strengthened in better times. Kevin Hurley posits a rationale for a learning society, reviews the Green Paper and reflects a vigilant optimism in this sector. The tradition of trade union involvement in members' education is highlighted by Peter Cassells who identifies barriers to mature student participation at third-level and stresses ICTU's priority to have such barriers removed.

In Eamon Gilmore's view, education's reluctance to change outdated practices and expectations may have profound implications for the future of our schools. Micheál Martin's reflections on the advent of the learning society also stress a growth beyond traditional schooling.

These chapters are not just a snapshot in time of the Irish education system; they are a frame from a moving picture, one vivified and expanded by the perspectives, insights and aspirations of people who care deeply about that system. The sum of the parts of this book is a record of some key developments over the years, an assessment of the health of the education service, and an agenda of issues facing policy-makers, practitioners and students early in the twenty-first century. It is a timely and relevant reminder of the centrality of education in determining what kind of society we will bequeath to the next generation.

In Memory of Michael Enright

1

To Be A Child

Philomena Donnelly

Some years ago, a young child fell into a gorilla pit at Bristol
Zoo. As the child lay unconscious a female gorilla who had recently given birth stood over him, gently stroking his head and
chasing off other gorillas until help arrived. The instinct to protect our young is very strong. How we treat our young says a
lot about us. In this I am not commenting on how individual
parents treat their particular children but how as a society we
view children. Some would claim that any society can be
judged on how it treats its very young and very old — the most
vulnerable in our communities.

According to the 1996 census there are 305,557 children under the age of six in Ireland. Where are these children? What
do we know of their daily lives?

In a capitalist society, such as our own, children are of no
value. They have no power, they own no wealth and they are of
no exchange value. So basically they count for little. On the
other hand, we supposedly live in a democratic capitalist society which should care for all its citizens.

At present three different reports are with the Government
all relating to the welfare, care and education of young children:

• *Report of the Commission on the Family* (1998)

- *Report on the National Forum for Early Childhood Education* (1998)

- *The Partnership 2000 Expert Working Group on Childcare* (1999).

In this article I will look at the reality of life for young children in Ireland today through the research available and by reflecting on some of the children I have taught over many years.

The 1991 Childcare Act places a statutory duty on health boards to identify and promote the welfare of children, as well as to provide a range of childcare and family support services. In reality, most health boards are finding it increasingly difficult to fulfil their statutory role because of inadequate funding. Ireland, with its booming economy, now has the distinction of having the second highest level of child poverty in the European Union (*Eurostat*, 1997 (6)). According to the Combat Poverty Agency report on *Child Poverty in Ireland* (Nolan and Farrell, 1990), the more children families have the greater the risk of poverty. Callan and Nolan (1991) define poverty:

> a person is in poverty when, due to lack of resources, he or she is excluded from the ordinary living patterns, customs and activities in the society.

Thus, poverty is seen and understood in the context of the ordinary living patterns of a particular society and is, therefore, relative. One aspect that the reports establish is that the risk of poverty has increased much faster for children than for adults. So my assertion that children are of no value in a capitalist society is not true. Children, and the number of them, can have a direct correlation with poverty. They are of value — a negative value.

> The scale of a family's disadvantage will depend on the age and number of children (Callan and Nolan, 1991).

Children in Irish society have become a liability. In *Educational Disadvantage in Ireland* (1995) the Combat Poverty Agency points out that young people from socially and economically deprived backgrounds benefit substantially less from educational expenditure than those from better-off backgrounds. Rather than enhancing children's opportunities, in reality school in many cases marginalises the children of the poor who tend to leave school as soon as they can with little more than an abiding sense of failure. The education system reinforces privilege.

> Is there a solution to this dysfunction of education systems, which throughout the world almost always proclaim equality of chances and yet manage to favour the children of the elite? (Combat Poverty Agency, 1995).

Since the 1960s there have been a number of intervention programmes with limited success. Of much interest now are the Early Start Programme and the Breaking the Cycle Programme. Thirty-three urban schools and 123 rural schools are in the Breaking the Cycle Programme. The Early Start is attached to 40 schools covering 1,680 children in Dublin, Cork, Limerick, Galway, Waterford, Drogheda and Dundalk. In total 318 schools have been designated as disadvantaged. Such programmes provide improved teacher–pupil ratios, increased capitation grants and grants for materials and equipment. Parental involvement is encouraged.

I am not a child. Have you ever wondered what it is like to be a child now? Sometimes it is difficult to see and understand legislation out of context. I would like to introduce you to some of the children I have come to know through teaching over the past 24 years.

In Belfast I met Robert. He left a lasting impression on me because he contradicted a great many of the educational theo-

ries I had been taught in college. He was from a working class background in Lenadoon in West Belfast. He came from a home with little, if any, reading material and not a lot of income. He was, at age four, one of those little fellas who seem to be bursting through their skin, as if their skin is behind their bone and body growth. Kojak was a major TV programme at the time. It was the wish of every child in my class to have their hair shaved. Parental disapproval was easily circumvented. The boys with head lice became very popular and in huge demand. Heads would be rubbed together and tight embraces endured to ensure the jump was made. After a few days scratching a Kojak hair-do followed. These were a class of four- to five-years-olds. My first lesson: never underestimate the imagination or the determination of children when they are stimulated by interest. However, back to Robert.

After the initial stages of pre-reading had been covered, I introduced Robert to his first reader with the first four pages to be read. Next morning in school he approached me. "Miss, do you remember that there wee book you gave me?" I said that I did, to which he replied, "Well, if I give it back to you will you give me another one?"

In my best teacher manner I explained gently to him that I'd love to give him another "wee book" but he'd have to read the one he had first. He told me he could read it. Presuming his understanding of reading to be different from mine, I asked him to bring it up. And he read it. I gave him another book and he read it over the next night. The child just read. With enthusiasm and with interest he read and he read. I didn't always have time during class to keep up with him. As the infants went home earlier than the older boys I told him he could stay after school to do extra reading if he wished. So he did and, over the rest of that year, an average of ten boys — different ones on different days — would stay behind to do more reading. The motivation and the initiative came from Robert. It was my second year teaching. I received a great deal of advice and assistance from the staff of the school but my first class of infants taught me a lot. I remember other little incidents about that year 1975/76. The children had no real concept of a policeman as they had never seen one. Also, one morning one of them came through the classroom door and announced: "Miss, my granny died but she wasn't shot."

I often wonder what happened to Robert and his friends. Did some of them make it through? Did they make the system work for them or did it isolate and "fail" them?

In 1977 I moved to Dublin to teach in the Rutland Pre-school Project. Never had I witnessed poverty on such a scale as I encountered in Dublin's north inner city. It was my first real experience of the pain of childhood. I met many happy and energetic children but I also came to know children who, I have no doubt now, were suffering from depression. One little girl, Alice, would sit, uninterested, her eyes heavy and her body lethargic. I tried to coax her into making a jigsaw with me. Not lacking ability in terms of understanding, she wearily put one piece of the jigsaw into place. It was coming up to Christmas and to engage her in conversation I asked her what Santa would be bringing her. At three years of age she looked at me and said, "he won't come". I cajoled her and reassured her that of course he'd come. She patiently repeated, "he won't come". In my clumsiness I tried again. With a sigh of exasperation she looked at me directly and repeated, "he won't come; the Vincents come". She was referring to the Society of St Vincent de Paul. As part of my teaching, I was involved in some home/school liaison work on different days and by arrangement I went home with different children. On that day I would bring them home from school. Alice was very thrilled on the day I was going home with her. She skipped and chatted all the way to the top of Sean McDermott Street where it met Gardiner Street. This was before both streets had the old houses knocked down. We climbed the stairs to the very top where Alice pushed against a sheet of zinc, which was the family's front door and brought me into their living room. There were ten children in this family. I have never seen anything in real life as close to a scene from a Beckett play as the furnishing of that room. There were four chairs, one table and a tin of peas. There was nothing else in the room. No bits and pieces lying around. Some of the children were rolling the tin of peas up and down the table. Bare walls, bare floor. The only decoration or colour was the tin of peas. Alice's mother invited me to sit on one of the chairs and pleasantly talked about the children and their education and I thought of Alice's patience with me in school. A family who had learned to survive by being patient with the "experts" around them. It was the worst case of poverty I came across in my two years teaching there.

I remember another waif-like little girl, Jenny, whose Mam sold papers outside Arnotts in Henry Street. The mother had a great big pram into which went the papers and the current baby. Language development was a major aspect of the curriculum and I will always remember Jenny's ability to say in a deep and strong voice with very definite intonation, "Herald or Press".

What Now for the Children of These Children?

Health boards themselves have new powers to become directly involved in the provision of services in areas where there is a low level of activity. In 1994 the Department of Social Community and Family Affairs funded 45 Family Resource Centres with crèche and other services for the under-six-year-olds to help combat disadvantage. Rural poverty and disadvantage is also something that needs to be addressed. The Western and Mid-Western Health Boards have grant-aided schemes such as CLARECARE, which provides early childhood services in parts of Galway, Mayo and Roscommon. These are often attached to local primary schools.

The National Anti-Poverty Strategy 1997 recommends the provision of specific intervention programmes designed to address educational disadvantage and the phased extension of the Early Start Programme. The strategy would encourage the increase of pre-school services in partnership with community interests.

Are these intervention programmes working? Are they fulfilling the objectives they set out with? An evaluation of the Early Start Programme (1998), while not detecting discernible cognitive gains for the Programme's participants, recorded positive outcomes related to parental engagement and satisfaction with the Programme, the children's positive attitude to school, ease in adaptation to the junior infant classroom and confidence towards schooling (*Report of the National Forum on Early Childhood Education*, 1998, p. 80).

Longitudinal studies in the US have shown that the High/Scope Pre-school Programme has saved taxpayers seven dollars for every dollar invested in the Programme for disadvantaged children. The savings were in terms of the cost of juvenile delinquency, remedial education, income support and joblessness (Schweinhart and Weikart, 1993).

Barnardos have introduced this programme in their facility in Millbrook in Tallaght. From the American research it would appear that it is during adolescence that the benefit of such programmes can be realised in areas such as achievement, motivation and social behaviour.

The 305,557 children under the age of six in Ireland all matter. Childcare and child education must be universal.

> Apart from child benefit and limited interventions for children at risk of social or educational disadvantage, there is virtually no State investment in the care of chil-

dren in the years before entry to primary school (Commission on the Family, 1998).

The one thing all three reports emphasise is the lack of co-ordination of what services are there. They are patchy and there is no cohesion. The recommendations of the Report on Early Childhood Education are well worth considering and acting on. One of the main recommendations is for a comprehensive policy on the early years. At present provision is fragmented, inadequate and in many areas absent altogether. Participants at the Forum held in Dublin Castle in February 1998 emphasised that while early childhood systems can and should achieve several goals, a primary objective would be to respond to the actual needs of young children, especially those living in precarious circumstances. The Report recommends the setting up of an Early Years Development Unit to be located jointly in the Department of Health and Children and the Department of Education and Science, with the former being the lead department for the under-three-year-olds and the latter taking the lead for the four-to-six-year age group.

The Partnership 2000 Expert Working Group on Childcare calls for the registering of child minders and a system of tax relief towards childminding costs, childminding subsidies for people on low incomes and grants and subsidies for childcare providers.

There are two vital questions here:

1. When will the Government act and introduce legislation based on the three reports?

2. Is the motivation for such action coming more from the demands of having women return to the workforce rather than the needs of children?

If it is coming from the demands of such bodies as the Irish Business and Employers' Confederation (IBEC) to fill the jobs, then I'm wrong again. Children can be of value in a capitalist society as they are potential workers. What is happening to childhood? These are the political and ethical issues that need to be discussed and understood so that any forthcoming legislation will be child-centred.

In 1979, following declining numbers in Rutland Street, I moved to Bayside Junior School in Sutton. A very well equipped school in a middle class area. It was simply a different world but with one distinct thing in common — children. I've put hundreds of children under the age of eight through my hands. I have spent 24 years working full-time with children, each of them an individual. I have often worried for them and about them but never when I'm with them. Their buoyancy for life is infectious. I have shared their thoughts, their dreams, their imaginations, their excitements, their sadness, their humour and their courage. Making sense of this world is not an easy task. It can be an enjoyable journey. You can't hand a child a made world. They have to make it their own. Understanding comes from within. I would now like to share with you some of the children's understanding of this world from doing philosophy with them.

When did time begin? November 1995:

"Time started when dreams came true."

Pictures, June 1995:

"Pictures die when they go in the bin; when they're made; sometimes pictures go to sleep when people go to sleep and wake up when people wake up."

"Sometimes when you are bold to people and say they can't draw a nice picture, you hurt the people's feelings. In the whole wide world that's the boldest word you've ever heard."

"So when pictures are drawn they can go through your head; it doesn't matter if they go in the bin. It's really awful to scribble on a picture — red, like blood — they don't like it. They don't like to be torn up or cut up too fast. They want to play."

"Pictures come alive when you don't tear them or throw them in the bin. You can keep pictures in your mind and keep drawing them and drawing them."

"Pictures are very happy when you keep them in your mind because they know you love them if you keep them in your mind."

The Tooth Fairy, May 1996:

"The tooth fairy; you see they want your teeth so they make their toys out of them; that's why they give you money."

"The tooth fairy has no teeth and loads of money. They give you money for your teeth."

"I wonder how fairies get money because if they have no teeth how could they get money?"

"I wonder why the tooth fairy doesn't wake you up and give you the money?"

"I really wonder where she gets the money from?"

"'I wonder; my Mam works in a bank and she never sees a tooth fairy."

Why are people different colours? October 1995:

"People are different colours because born in different countries."

"When trees are different colours, people are different colours."

"It depends on what country and what temperature."

"If people are black and white why can't they be red or blue?"

"Leaves have different colours."

In writing this article I thought a great deal about the title. I chose "To Be A Child" because I am concerned that in the million or so words written in the three reports that are now with the Government there is a danger of the central focus being lost. I would like if in some way members of the Dáil could reflect on what it is like to be a child in the 1990s in Ireland. That is not one thing. For the under-sixes it is 305,557 things. I would encourage them to talk to and listen to young children, to visit crèches and playgroups and infant classes in primary schools. The whole question of the care and education of our young begs us to reflect on the society and the values we are offering to them. In dealing with children there is and always will be a need to offer a variety of services and flexibility within them. The workplace is becoming more and more dehumanised. Those working in the caring professions are acting counter-culture. This question of the care and education of our young and how we view childhood will tell us a great deal about ourselves.

We must act now on the reports. Radicals and humanists must claim the central ground and ensure that legislation and action are child-centred and not market-driven.

[All the names of the children referred to in this article have been changed to protect their privacy.]

References

Callan, T., Nolan, B., et al. (1991), *Poverty, Income and Welfare in Ireland*, Dublin: ESRI.

Census of Population (1996), Dublin: Central Statistics Office.

Commission on the Family (1998), *Strengthening Family Life: Executive Summary of Final Report*.

Educational Disadvantage in Ireland (1995), Dublin: Department of Education, Combat Poverty Agency and Educational Research Centre.

Nolan, B., Farrell, B. (1990), *Child Poverty in Ireland*, Dublin: Combat Poverty Agency.

Report on the National Forum for Early Childhood Education (1998), Dublin: Government Publications.

Schweinhart, L.J., et al. (1993), *Significant Benefits: The High / Scope Perry Pre-School Study Through Age 27*, Michigan High/Scope Education Research Foundation.

2

Getting the Basics Right

Joe O'Toole

Recently there has been much focus on the area of childcare. We see emerging more official interest, more regulations and generally more concern. As a result of one directive regarding the level of care and requirements in terms of the ratio of children to adult minders many crèches have had either to close down or to up their prices in order to employ more staff. All very well and all very welcome except that in some cases the four-year-olds leaving the crèche are being sent to the local primary school where they are liable to be in a class of up to 35 or more infants. It is quite incredible that, while the law of the land requires one adult minder to every eight children in crèches, up to 35 or 40 children of the same age in a primary school infant class does not even raise an official eyebrow.

This cannot and will not last.

Therefore, the most significant development due to change the shape and architecture of Irish primary education in the 2000s will be welcome advances in the area of early childhood education. There will be a shake-up of infant education and of pre-schools. This will be the result of a number of objectives and concerns of disparate groups coinciding for positive results. Teachers have long felt that the support for the younger child, particularly in the infant classes, has been abysmally deficient. Parents continue to demand better and improved surroundings for their young children whether in playgroups, pre-schools or infant classes. Women's groups are insisting on State-supported childcare in order to support mothers who wish to return and participate in the workforce. Trade unions are pressurising Government for proper regulation of the conditions in which young children are babysat, supervised or taught. Taxpayers are screaming for tax breaks to compensate for child-minding costs. And employers — not for any social or caring reason, but because skill and labour shortages are threatening productivity and profits, and because they must therefore both maintain parents in the workforce and attract them back to it — are finally supporting the thrust of the demands from teachers, parents, unions and taxpayers.

In recent times two reports have been published which are central to this debate. They are the *Early Childhood Education Report* (1998) and the *Report of the Commission on Childcare* (1999). These must surely be the catalyst to a new beginning in education. It will require creativity, flexibility and visionary leadership to bring together the many interest and pressure groups in a manner which ensures that all the varied and various cogs engage to advance provision for young children in or out of school. The challenge will be to ensure that the different interest groups identify common issues and advance them co-operatively.

For instance, primary education deals with children from age four whereas early childhood provision will be targeted at children up to the age of five. There is obviously an overlap. It would be confusing to say the least if the specifications and the safety requirements of the buildings, the qualifications of the adults in charge or the learning structures envisaged did not complement each other whether the child is in a primary school infant class, a pre-school or a crèche.

A number of developments in recent times will facilitate these matters. The acceptance by the Minister for Education of a proposal that the terms of reference of the National Council for Curriculum and Assessment (NCCA) should be extended to include early childhood education was reflected in an amendment to the Education Act (1998) which has now given legislative authority to this change. The fact that the National Council for Education Awards (NCEA) has validated one of the four-year Montessori courses as a degree course and that the conditions for extending its recognition in primary education are under active consideration among the Department, the INTO and the NCEA, is more than a straw in the wind. The move towards a national qualification, awarded after not less than two years' full-time study for those working with teachers in the early childhood area, is significant. The offer of a post-graduate diploma in early childhood education by at least one College of Education is yet another sign of the broadening of interest in the professionalisation of this aspect of education. All in all, there is an inexorable movement towards a fuller service for pupils up to the age of five.

Getting the basics right will be the name of the game. All learning and education must be structured. The NCCA will be required to come up with a vital and relevant curriculum for this age group and one which will allow the child to progress seamlessly and effortlessly on to the primary school programme. Delivering this effectively will be a matter for trained and qualified professionals. Working on the basis that "the younger the child the more specialised the teaching" it will be necessary to ensure that the youngest children be exposed only to the most qualified personnel. The personnel can of course be varied. Any group (even the INTO) arguing that only one kind of qualification, primary teacher for instance, be acceptable to teach at this level should be disregarded. Here we need variety. We will certainly need primary teachers but we must also see, and welcome enthusiastically, the valuable contribution qualified childcare workers can make. There must also be a role for the trained teacher who has gone on to specialise and gain further qualification in the early childhood level, and most crucially there must be a more open space for parental involvement than is the case in any other sector of education. It is exciting to envisage this type of development with busy children and a productive interaction between professionals and parents in a comfortable building.

In some cases this will be attached to the local primary school; in other cases it will be a stand-alone community initiative. Whichever it be, the challenge to all of us will be to maintain a quality service.

The millennium will bring with it a new flexibility of approach which is growing and permeating through all aspects of society. Let us hope that primary education will not be excluded from these winds of change. The need for more diversity in education will be accepted when professional, economic and social objectives coincide. At primary level this will bring a revolution in the manner in which teachers attain pre-service qualifications. There will certainly be the traditional route through the colleges of education with students pursuing a concurrent programme comprising professional, academic and practical aspects. More and more, however, there will be teachers coming via the post-graduate course having already graduated with a basic degree in a subject which need not necessarily include education. But this will not be the end of it; undoubtedly there will be new routes. I fully expect that very soon we will have conversion courses for qualified post-primary teachers to transfer to primary and vice versa. As soon as we have agreed and established the qualification for education personnel at early childhood level we will no doubt have to consider conversion courses for them if they wish to be qualified for all of the primary age range. The European Union's directive on the mutual recognition of third level professional qualifications will also lead to changes and will probably result in some relaxation in the Irish language qualifications for teacher entrants from outside the State. We have recently seen other moves to relax such requirements.

In truth there is no area of education which will not change during the first decade of the new millennium. The same would be true of the next decade even if it were not in a new century. In point of fact we should, in the spirit of pluralism and inclusiveness, move away from the notion that time began or changed with the birth in Bethlehem. The logical position is that a new millennium begins with every annual orbit of the sun. Every year begins a new millennium and with it should come the excitement of change and innovation. In education, change should be the rule rather than the exception. Next January begins just another year. It is hardly worth waiting for; let's do it now!

References

Report on the National Forum for Early Childhood Education (1998), Dublin: Government Publications.

Partnership 2000 Expert Working Group on Childcare (1999) Dublin: Government Publications.

3

Quality — the Key Debate in Education

Richard Bruton

The education system has expanded rapidly in the last 20 years. In that period the proportion of the age cohort sitting their Leaving Certificate has risen from 60 per cent to 80 per cent. The numbers qualifying from third-level colleges have increased even more dramatically from 15 per cent to 50 per cent. Post Leaving Certificate courses, which were non-existent in the early 1980s, now attract a further 20 per cent of the cohort.

This radical expansion in participation in education has been a hugely significant investment from a national point of view. Parents and taxpayers alike made a major investment during the lean 1980s and thereby laid the foundation for the current economic success.

Challenge Ahead

Education has now moved into a far more central position in dictating the economic success of nations. Mobile foreign investment now quickly moves in pursuit of skilled people. It is the capacity to innovate that determines success as old technologies are quickly imitated by emerging nations snapping at the heels of countries like Ireland.

Equally at a personal level, education has become the key gateway to economic success. Those who fall by the wayside in education are far more marginalised now than they ever were before. Education has become a lifelong challenge. But those who get a bad start are likely to fall further and further behind.

Education is thus becoming the most important policy instrument in pursuit of both economic success and of social justice. Providing a good education base is a highly effective method of tackling poverty. The global economy has loosened the grip of traditional forms of privilege and education is the foundation of an emerging meritocracy. However, it is abundantly obvious that public policy in education has dismally failed to even up life's chances.

Schools are clearly in a more pivotal role than they ever previously occupied. They are also being asked to take on more and more responsibility in helping young people cope with the more complex pressures of the modern world. Schools are expected to take on new roles and cope with issues such as substance abuse, sexual relationships and personal crises.

The traditional role of the schoolteacher is also changing in the face of new technologies. Schoolteachers are no longer the main fount of knowledge — imparting from their precious stock to attentive pupils. Now information and communication technology makes access to information simple. The real challenge is how to organise and use this information, how to learn to learn. The teacher's role is becoming one of facilitator and the skills of communication, leadership, planning and evaluation are becoming the essential stock-in-trade.

Many schools and teachers are poorly equipped to meet these changes.

Time for a New Debate

Often the debate in Ireland about education is very sterile. There is an almost exclusive emphasis on inputs rather than outcomes. The major debate focuses on issues such as the level of capitation, the pupil–teacher ratio, and the ex quota allocations rather than on school attendance, suspensions, literacy standards, and personal fulfilment.

To a large extent these outcomes have been taken for granted. This orientation towards inputs is not surprising in a system for which the main preoccupation for twenty years has been the rapid expansion of participation. However, now that we have reached internationally quite high levels of participation, we must look more carefully at quality issues.

When you shine the light into the darker corners of our education system some hard realities loom out of the shadows. More than one in six of our school leavers cannot carry out even the most basic literacy tasks, such as reading and understanding the back of an aspirin package.

It is no accident that people are often unaware of these very real problems in our education system. The government has in fact collected no information about crucial aspects of our education such as literacy and numeracy in schools, truancy and suspension, and about the special needs of children which require appropriate resources.

Our education system has been far from successful with pupils "who are from the back of the class". Early school leaving in Ireland is much higher than among comparable advanced countries.

Improving the quality of outcomes for such individuals is not just a matter of pumping more resources into the system. The quality of what is done is also crucial. The extent to which weaker pupils succeed in school is very much influenced by:

- The sort of policies a school pursues

- The sort of teaching methods applied by a school

- The type of curriculum and examination system which is in place

- The linkages that have been forged with the wider community.

Quality Improvement and Professional Development

As we approach the new millennium, the key education debate must be about quality. The quality of an education system is not measured by the volume of inputs but by the outcomes for pupils. Quality improvement must go to the heart of school management in the coming years. It will involve systematic analysis of what a school does — benchmarking against other players and reorganising work so that the school operates as a more cohesive team to improve results. This process can engage people in a new way — encouraging innovation, team working and taking new responsibility. Debate must move far beyond the old-fashioned quality control approach that has typified this debate in the UK. There, the emphasis has been on inspection and identifying unacceptable levels of failure. Irish teachers have reacted against the crude league tables that this approach produced.

The education system is the fountainhead from which excellence in other endeavours springs and it has even more reason to put quality improvement procedures in place. However, quality management seems to be viewed by many in the education system as something threatening rather than fulfilling. There has been a reluctance to participate in even the timid pilot Whole School Evaluation programme.

We shall never get to grips with the problems of educational disadvantage in this country unless we are willing to face up honestly to the obstacles encountered by such children both within and outside the school.

Schools must start to set themselves targets, apply best practice and monitor what they are achieving. Central to any process of improvement must be the generation of meaningful measures of performance and comparison.

It is strange that it is often those who are most eloquent in their advocacy of equality of outcomes from education, who are also the most resistant to the evaluation of these differences at school level.

The teaching profession should see the new emphasis on quality as central not only to better outcomes for pupils but also as central to the further development and improvement of their profession.

Ireland has been extraordinarily negligent in investing in our teaching force. Where private companies are happy to spend 5 per cent of payroll on the development of skills, the State spends less than 1 per cent on the development of the skills of teachers. The pursuit of a quality agenda will bring new responsibilities to the teaching profession. It will also open the gateway to better working conditions and better rewards.

Matching Institutional Change

Educational structures at primary and secondary level have been virtually unchanged over the past 60 years. They are characterised by a highly centralised Department of Education controlling all policy and resource allocation decisions on the one hand and, on the other, isolated schools operating almost entirely on their own.

This model is ill-equipped to deal with the challenges that now face education. Schools are expected to take on new roles but they have not been adequately equipped to do so. They are overstretched in managing day-to-day affairs and have little time for crucial innovation and development. Support services are thin on the ground and poorly integrated into the school setting. Co-operation between schools is poorly developed, as are links between the schools and the wider community.

The Department's policy approach tries to accommodate a huge variety of local needs within a small number of central-ised programmes. This is a "one-size-fits-all" approach to edu-cation. It just will not work for the future.

Now is the time to look at change in our system of education delivery. The Department needs to devolve power down to local level and be willing to resource strategies that are designed within the schools and between clusters of schools.

Schools, too, must look outward at the wider community and participate with other schools in joint activities and peer re-views. Area-based policies for education must begin to emerge and the community must have a chance to make a real input into the sort of policies that are pursued.

It is time for the Department of Education and Science to restructure itself. We need a dynamic Education Development Authority that can work with schools to innovate and develop new approaches. We need a Department that develops strong policy-making capability — the ability to evaluate policies, to learn from best practice overseas and to guide local innovation.

Just as the decisions over decades have laid the foundation for present economic success, so too will the decisions we take now about education determine our success in the new millen-nium.

4

Inclusiveness in Education

Áine Hyland

It is timely as we approach the third millennium to address the issue of inclusiveness in education. Concern with educational inclusiveness is a very recent phenomenon from a historical perspective. The concept of schooling for all, or "mass education", is a relatively recent one, dating back no more than 200 years in most western countries. From the beginning of the nineteenth century to the middle of the twentieth century, such mass schooling was very limited indeed and usually consisted of four or five years of elementary schooling. Second-level schooling for all is a phenomenon of our own lifetime and mass third-level education is only beginning to peep over the horizon.

Inclusiveness in education was not an issue which concerned educational thinkers and policy makers for the most part of the first two millennia. Western education traditions and practices have been strongly influenced by the social and educational philosophies of ancient Greece dating back 2,500 years. Plato's ideas of social organisation as outlined in his *Republic* contributed significantly to the development of the modern democratic state. Broadly speaking, Plato envisaged the state as consisting of Rulers (with legislative and deliberative functions); Auxiliaries (with executive functions); and

Craftsmen (with productive functions). The institution of the state would be based, not on birth or wealth, but on natural capacities and attainments. Education would play an important role in selecting and preparing those who would fill the various roles. (The labouring work would be done by slaves who would require no education!)

The notion of specialisation and separateness was fundamental to Plato's organisation and structure. In his ideal state, specific tasks would be allocated to specific people. He wrote: "We shall need at least one man to be a farmer, another a builder, and a third a weaver." And he added: "No two people are born exactly alike. There are innate differences which fit them for different occupations."

Throughout the western world, most schooling systems reflected, and continue to reflect, some aspects of Greek educational philosophy. Until the eighteenth century, education was available, generally speaking, only for the select few. While some countries attempted to include an element of meritocracy in their selection mechanisms, the more common model of selection was based on class and/or wealth, thus ensuring that power would continue to be held over time by the same families and dynasties. The influence of Plato and other Greek philosophers on democratic society today, and particularly on schooling, should not be underestimated. Inclusiveness was far from the concerns of these early educationalists. On the contrary, their philosophies led to exclusivity and selection and a conviction that the innate differences referred to by Plato could be identified and enhanced by appropriate education.

Why, then, was there a move towards mass education about 200 years ago? As is so often the case, the new thrust emerged from economic and industrial needs rather than from new philosophical/psychological insights. Towards the end of the eighteenth century the need for widespread literacy became more pressing in industrialised societies where mass production was becoming the norm. While the old apprenticeship system of training young people for trades and occupations continued to have its value, it was seen as an inadequate means of preparing large numbers of young people for the new industrial workforce of the eighteenth and nineteenth centuries. Schooling also had a social function, particularly in cities and large towns where law and order were matters of concern. Schools would keep poor children off the streets, would inculcate values and norms which would make them good citizens and would attempt to make them more productive members of the community.

Until very recently, mass schooling was concerned with providing basic or elementary education. It was important not to over-educate, nor to give children or young people aspirations which might be above their station in life. As well as teaching literacy, numeracy and the skills of penmanship schools sought to instil the social values of conformity, obedience and acceptance of the social order. For over a century after the introduction of mass schooling in the early decades of the nineteenth century, schooling at all levels continued to be socially selective and divisive. For example, in Ireland the national schools, started in 1831, were designed for "the education of the poor". Until the middle of the twentieth century, children of middle and upper class families did not attend national schools — they attended private primary or preparatory schools or were educated at home by tutors. Secondary education was unapologetically selective and exclusive from the start. Only a tiny proportion of the population attended Irish secondary schools during the nineteenth and early twentieth centuries. It has been estimated that when the Free State was founded in 1922, less than one in ten of those in their early teens attended any form of second-level education and less than one per cent completed secondary schooling. Even in the 1960s only a minority of young people (44 per cent) completed junior cycle second-level education.

Throughout the first six decades of the twentieth century, second-level education was provided on a dual basis — pupils attended either secondary schools or technical/vocational schools. Those who attended secondary schools could remain for five years, sit the Leaving Certificate and compete for a wide range of further educational and career/professional options. Those who attended vocational schools could only take advantage of a two-year course leading to the Group Certificate examination. There was no senior cycle education available for such pupils; on completion of the Group Certificate examination, they could either enter an apprenticeship or go directly to work.

Notions of equality of educational opportunity are very recent indeed. It is only in our lifetime, i.e. within the past 50 years, that second-level education for all has become the norm in the western world. And even then, equality of access was not envisaged. In most countries, until recently, young people were selected or "tracked" into either an academic or a vocational path. Entrance or transfer examinations at the end of primary school which purported to identify aptitude were used to allocate pupils to either the academic or the vocational track, although in practice these tests were tests of attainment, not of aptitude. This practice of selection and tracking at the end of primary school continues in some European countries, e.g. Northern Ireland, Germany and the Netherlands, to the present day. In most western countries, however, including Ireland, a more comprehensive and less specialised approach has been adopted at this level during the past 20 or 30 years, particularly for 12- to 15-year-olds.

Today there are 375,000 pupils enrolled in second-level schools in the Republic of Ireland, more than 208,000 of them at junior cycle level. Two-thirds of these are enrolled in secondary schools, over 25 per cent in vocational schools and the remainder in community and comprehensive schools. They are taught by a total of more than 20,000 teachers and all follow a broadly similar curriculum leading to the same examination at the end of the three-year course. The gradual move towards comprehensivisation of second-level education during the 1970s and 1980s culminated with the introduction of the new Junior Certificate programme by Minister for Education, Mary O'Rourke, in 1989 for all pupils entering second-level schools in September of that year. The first Junior Certificate examination was held in 1992. The intention of the new programme was "to provide a programme which will encompass those skills and competencies to which all young people should have access as a right, together with qualities of creativity, initiative and enterprise which are now, more than ever, so important". The Junior Certificate programme was designed and was to be taught in accordance with educational objectives and methodology which are "appropriate to the interests, aptitude, and achievement of students at each level". It was also hoped that students would have "access to a valid educational experience in each curricular area within the context of a unified system of assessment and certification".

A decade after the introduction of the Junior Certificate programme we might well ask whether its aims have in fact been achieved. To some extent the structure of the programme has attempted to respond to the different needs and abilities of a variety of young people. For example, three subjects, Irish, English and Mathematics, are offered at three levels — foundation, ordinary and higher. On the other hand, by the mid-1990s it was realised that in spite of its efforts to be an inclusive programme there were still young people who had difficulty in coping with it. In response to the needs of these young people, the Junior Certificate School Programme (previously called the Junior Certificate Elementary Programme) was in-

troduced in 1996. The Junior Certificate School Programme is
an intervention designed to ensure that all young people can
benefit from their time in school through acknowledging and
rewarding their achievements. It is targeted at schools with a
serious problem in early school leaving. Preliminary experience
suggests that this programme is effective in motivating and
supporting young people, more of whom now successfully complete junior cycle than was the case before the Junior Certificate School Programme was introduced.

In spite of all the developments of the past three decades
there continues to be a significant number of young people who
feel excluded from the system. For example, during the first
half of the 1990s, over a quarter of the age cohort left school
each year with inadequate or no qualifications. In 1995, it was
estimated that:

- 1,000 young people did not transfer from primary to second-
  level education;

- 2,200 left second-level school with no qualification whatso-
  ever;

- 7,900 left school with Junior Certificate only, of whom
  2,000 failed to achieve at least five passes;

- 2,100 left school having completed the Junior Certificate
  with a vocational preparation course only;

- Around 7,200 did not achieve five passes in the Leaving
  Certificate.

A recent report shows that, in OECD countries generally,
higher levels of education attainment are clearly associated, for
individuals, with higher earnings, lower chances of unemployment and more skills that yield advantages to people as consumers and active citizens. For example, university educated
people in their thirties and early forties are up to five times

less likely to be unemployed than the average person in that age group. As regards earnings, university educated men and women earn more on average in mid-life than those with upper secondary education only. The situation is particularly marked in relation to women. University educated women earn 61 per cent more on average than those with upper secondary education only. At the other end of the scale, those who leave school early are particularly vulnerable to high unemployment. A 1994 OECD study stated that the evidence on youth employment in the 1980s and early 1990s showed that young people with inadequate skills and competencies face a growing threat of low income or complete economic marginalisation.

In terms of investment priorities in education in the future decade, it is clear that under-achievers and early school leavers must be high on the government's priority list. It is sobering to realise that a child who leaves the education system after primary school has had only £11,400 spent on them by the State. This compares with £15,850 spent on the pupil who leaves after two years of secondary school and is in sharp contrast to the £37,525 spent by the State on a student who completes a four year programme at third level. In terms of minimum equity, it is reasonable to ask that priority be given to investment in the first group of young people. A recent OECD report suggests that policies to increase equity and efficiency in education and training should consider carefully not only the incentives for pursuing on-going study but also the quality of and attitudes to learning in the lifelong perspective. Such policies should ensure that young people gain positive and constructive experiences of learning in school on which they can continue to build through adulthood. If school has been an unhappy and demotivating experience for young people, it is unlikely that they will be willing to pursue education on a lifelong basis. Some of the practices which are taken for granted in our schooling system have done nothing but confirm the feelings of failure of some young people and have alienated them from the education system. Norm-referenced tests, which of their nature identify "successful" and "failing" pupils, can do nothing to affirm those young people who always end up at the bottom of the so-called ability pile. If intelligence continues to be defined and measured in a linear norm-referenced way, then there is no way up for those who are told repeatedly that they are unintelligent and failures.

The theory of multiple intelligences, first proposed by Howard Gardner in the US in 1983, is a direct challenge to the classical view of intelligence. Gardner defines an intelligence as "the ability to solve problems or fashion products that are of consequence in a particular cultural setting or community". According to Gardner, there are at least eight relatively autonomous but inter-connected intelligences. These include:

- Linguistic
- Logical-mathematical
- Spatial
- Bodily-kinaesthetic
- Musical
- Naturalist
- Interpersonal
- Intrapersonal.

He sees intelligence not as a fixed and measurable entity but rather as "a potential, the presence of which allows an individual access to forms of thinking appropriate to specific kinds of content". The recognition of a multiplicity of intelligences requires that teachers recognise a diversity of learner styles and these must be responded to appropriately. Preliminary findings from research on the application of multiple intelligences strategies in classrooms suggests that it leads to increased pupil motivation and a greater sense of excitement and involvement in one's own learning.

The exclusive origins of secondary education in Ireland continue to be manifest in the underpinning philosophy and organisation of many of our schools. For example, a small number of secondary schools in Ireland continue to be fee-paying schools and, therefore, accessible only to a relatively small number of wealthy families. The legacy of exclusiveness is also seen in the strong tendency at second-level schools to stream pupils within schools and often within classes. Schools would argue that it makes sense to keep students of similar achievement levels together and yet one might question what achievement is being measured and how is it being measured? Schools have traditionally rewarded only two of the intelligences set out by Gardner — the linguistic and the logical-mathematical. Grouping low-achieving pupils together in one stream is usually a self-fulfilling prophecy. We now know that pupils in the lower streams achieve less well in State and other examinations than similar ability students in mixed-ability classes. On the other hand, there is no evidence that streaming improves the achievement of pupils in higher stream classes. The grouping together of students of low levels of achievement has been found to have negative effects on students' motivation and so is likely to reinforce, rather than solve, the problems of pupils from disadvantaged backgrounds. Young people who associate school with continuing failure will be more likely to leave school early and are unlikely to be enthusiastic about opportunities for lifelong learning.

While much has been done during the past few decades to develop a culture of greater inclusivity within our schools and within our education system, much still remains to be done. The challenge ahead is considerable for schools, teachers, parents, employers and policy-makers. The current economic boom in Ireland owes a lot to the investment in education of successive governments during the past 30 years or so. Many of us contributing to this commemorative project and many of the readers of this publication have been beneficiaries of this investment but there are still too many in this country who have remained unaffected by the investment. The key priority for governments as we move into the twenty-first century has to be the development of a more inclusive system where no person is an outsider and where equal opportunities for success and achievement, defined in an inclusive and holistic way, are available for all.

5

School is Becoming a Thing of the Past

Eamon Gilmore

We have inherited our education system from the last century. It will not survive the next. Our primary schools owe their origins to the education reforms of the early nineteenth century; and the second-level school has, apart from curriculum, hardly changed at all in the past hundred years.

The concept of school itself is the product of industrial society. The school is the educational replica of the industrial age factory. Its hierarchical structure; the master/servant nature of the teacher pupil relationship and its archaic rules are becoming irrelevant and inappropriate in the Information age. It will be out of date in the twenty-first century.

The strains are already showing. Discipline is now the biggest daily challenge facing most teachers. The pupils are not more unruly than before, but relative to other attractions, school has become a more boring place.

The classroom was once the only, or at least the principal, source of information, learning and intellectual stimulation for the child. This is no longer the case. Now the school is competing with television, computers, the internet and a more informed social milieu for the child's attention. The child wants to be entertained. The school is not a playhouse and the teacher is a not a stand-up comic! In many schools, the teacher is doing well to teach for 15 minutes in a 40-minute class period. The rest of the time they are simply trying to keep order.

Yet school continues to be internally organised in a way which would not be unfamiliar to our great-great-grand parents. We still expect young adults, some of whom are now parents themselves, to show up for school, in dowdy (but expensive) uniforms, and to subject themselves to an authoritarian regime, which is designed to serve the institution rather than the student, and which has not adapted to a changed work and social environment.

It cannot last. The new century will bring huge changes to education. The school will be unrecognisable, if indeed it survives at all. As with all forms of change, the transformation in education can either be led and managed by the educationalists or it will be forced upon the system by the needs of the new society, which has now reached a higher stage of evolution than the school.

I suspect it will be the latter, because to date the "partners in education" show little enthusiasm for the kind of radical change which will happen one way or the other. The big problem is that forced change may result in an educational environment which none of us will like.

Some changes have been happening for some time, especially at third level and in the extension of second level into further education. Because of their closeness to the world of work, it is hardly surprising that it is the third level and further education sectors which have been first to respond. The influence has not been all in one direction. Education has also impacted on the industrial and business environment. For example, modern business, science and technology parks have the feel of a campus rather than an industrial estate.

Distance education, the Open University, the concept of Lifelong learning and the development of PLC and VTOS courses are examples of educationalists recognising the new market and the changing demands for an education service which is relevant to the growing and changing requirements of the economy.

However, mainstream second-level and first-level have been slower to adapt. To be fair to the primary level, it has been saddled with an impossible task. In theory there is a child-centred curriculum but this is difficult to teach in classes of over thirty pupils. The result is the worst of both worlds. The pupils neither learn the new curriculum for which small classes are essential, nor in many cases do they acquire the more traditional Three Rs. Many end up entering second level with a reading age three or four years behind their chronological age. This is no fault of the over-stretched teachers in the primary school, but of the unreasonable contradiction between their mandate and the resources with which they are equipped.

Additional resources may be the medicine for the primary school's ailment, but surgery will be necessary at second level. The crisis will come at senior cycle. For how much longer will 16-, 17- and 18-year-olds, who are adult in every other respect, continue to tolerate being treated as children by the school? Will they remain satisfied that it is school and not the pupils themselves which determines their subject choice options and the allocation of teachers to them?

Take a senior cycle student who has made a career choice, filled out the CAO form and knows roughly how many points they are going to need to get a college place. The student wants to take both chemistry and history at Leaving Certificate but in their school, chemistry and history are alternatives. They need chemistry for the third-level course and are good at history and want it for the points. Why should they have to choose, to their disadvantage, just to suit the school timetable? The other school in the town has a good history teacher. Why can't the student do history there? By what law must a student confine themselves to one school for all their subjects which are part of a national exam, and a national third-level selection process?

And if one can choose to study different subjects in different schools, why not have choice of teacher within the school? If, for example, a school has three English teachers, why should some pupils have inflicted on them the teacher who cannot control a class and who gets consistently bad results?

In every area of our market-led society, the consumer is supreme. How can the school hope to remain immune to the market? Already, grind schools and a variety of private exam-focused institutes have arrived to challenge the traditional second-level school.

Securing the points to get the first CAO choice is the priority. A good school may offer a well-rounded education by striking a balance between the academic, the extra-curricular and character formation but these days character is formed as much on the street as in the schoolyard; one can join a health club or a sports club for physical education or recreation, and socialising is more interesting anywhere else but in school.

The new century will begin with a growth in "no frills" schooling for Leaving Certificate candidates. In this affluent society more people will be able and willing to pay for it. The course-only school will appear to be better value for money than the prestigious fee-paying alma mater which may be good at rugby, but mediocre at winning points in the only league that really matters, the CAO. Good teachers will eventually be attracted out of mainstream schools by the rewards which market education will be prepared to offer, and in turn schools will have to respond by giving the consumer what he or she wants.

Before long, senior cycle schools will be offering not the full Leaving Certificate package but individual courses, the success or failure of which will ultimately be determined by consumer reputation. The senior cycle student will decide their own subjects and shop around for the best courses. The individual student may attend a number of schools of their own choice. Career guidance or counselling will probably be a service operated privately for which the student will pay a fee.

This scenario flies in the face of what most of us would consider a good and fair education system, and no doubt teacher unions and other educationalists would be first to challenge it. But the world is changing, and resistance today may become compliance tomorrow. Ten years ago who would have predicted that the workers in State-owned companies, who then railed against privatisation, would now be applauding the Minister who is selling off their company, for the very understandable reason that she is selling a big chunk of it to them?

The teacher unions may be today hostile to the marketisation of education, but give their members a slice of the action and all that will change. Already there is talk of private investment in the building and managing of school premises. If outsiders can make money out of education, why not those who are already working in it. If teachers start to see their own school as an investment opportunity and get the whiff of school ownership, the Churches may yet have more to fear from their own staff than from the State.

Education does not of course have to become a market commodity in the twenty-first century. Policy makers can anticipate and make provision for the changes and ensure that the service will be universally available, professionally delivered and democratically accountable.

However, this will require a fundamental reorganisation of the education service to meet the needs of the new century.

The assumptions about work on which our present system is based no longer apply. Traditionally it was taken that the individual finishes education before entering work, that the individual's career is in turn based on the educational level attained, and that they will remain in the same career, if not even the same job, for the extent of their working life.

This model of work is history. So too is the education frame on which it rests. In the new century the typical worker will require frequent returns to the classroom. The relationship between education and work will radically change and consequently the purely age-related education service we now have will become redundant.

Levels of educational attainment will be what matter. Has one mastered this level in order to move on to the next stage? The transfer, for example, from primary to second level will not automatically occur at age twelve and after sixth class irrespective of literacy and numeracy. Movement from one level of education to the next will only occur when the pupil has acquired the knowledge and skills to cope with and benefit from the next stage.

The stages of education themselves will radically change. The three levels of education which we have now will probably be replaced by at least five stages:

- A socialisation stage, offering pre-school education, typically between ages three and six;

- A numeracy and literacy stage, corresponding roughly to the present primary schooling, typically between ages six and eleven;

- A general education stage, overlapping the end of what is now sixth class in Primary School and the Junior Certificate and Transition Year Programmes. Typically this would last for four years;

- Senior school, which would lead to the Leaving Certificate or its equivalent and would be the preparation for Degree, Diploma or Certificate education. Students would have freedom of choice in subjects, teachers and the school for individual subjects;

- "Third-Level".

It can no longer be assumed that the typical worker undergoes education until they are in their early twenties, then works for forty years and thereafter draws a pension until death.

In the next century, the typical worker will probably return to education a number of times during their lifetime; will probably want to reduce work commitments during child-rearing (irrespective of gender); may wish to ease off on full time work in later life, but continue working to some extent beyond 65. All this has huge implications for student support, social welfare and pension policy, and these will need to be integrated.

In short, the basic social welfare payments will need to be paid to students throughout their fourth and fifth stages of education, regardless of the stage of life at which they undertake it. This payment can be assumed in the calculation of PRSI rates. The individual will receive social welfare payments while in education, but will contribute to it from his or her income.

Education will change dramatically in the next century. Whether the change results in a decent, accessible public service or a purely market driven product depends on how receptive to change are today's education partners.

The information age will have deeper implications for education than simply learning about and applying the new technologies. The question is, not how useful is the computer in the classroom but is the classroom any use at all in the age of the computer?

6

Teacher Professionalism in an Era of Change

Charles Lennon

> Entering the twenty-first century, the quality of Ire-
> land's human resources will be of central strategic
> importance in driving and underpinning competitiveness
> . . . with all other factors of production easily tradable,
> competitiveness will increasingly be dependent on the
> skill and creativeness of the Irish workforce.

The above quote is taken from the influential Forfás report on
the Irish economy, *Shaping Our Future: A Strategy for Enterprise in Ireland in the 21st Century* (Forfás, 1996). The key role
accorded to human resource development in this report is
echoed in virtually all of the many reports on the Irish and the
European economies in recent years. The forces at work in the
economies of the European Union have already been well
documented and include:

- Trends in the international pattern of economic development and trade

- The impact of technological change and the advent of the
  information society

- The structure and organisation of the workforce

- The pattern of demographic change

- The move towards EMU.

Education and training systems are universally regarded as being of critical importance in enabling countries of the European Union to meet and manage these changes. At a social and political level, intensive debates are underway in the EU institutions and the member states on the nature of social institutions, systems of social protections and the role of the State in social and economic life. At a more micro-level, there have also been profound changes in culture and in people's daily lives and expectations. Increasingly, citizens, whether as consumers of public or commercial services, want value for money, quality and accountability — especially when things go wrong — and are prepared to take legal action to receive what they regard as their entitlements. Concepts of ethnic and national identity are changing and many European societies are both multi-cultural and multi-ethnic. In this context, it is important that concepts of citizenship are consolidated. Binding concepts of citizenship are also important to counteract the frequently negative impact of individualism on social institutions such as the family and the local community. The concept of "social capital" in the sense of creating a social infrastructure and a "social" market is gaining increasing momentum as societies seek to maintain cohesion and meaning in this era of unparalleled economic and technological change.

In all of these projects, education is accorded a fundamental and pivotal role. Today's schools are, in addition to ensuring the delivery of a quality curriculum, expected to combat social disadvantage, provide children with the social skills and the self-esteem to say no to drugs and no to inappropriate sexual behaviour, prevent them from being victims of child abuse and inculcate values of tolerance and respect for diverse cultures. These examples are not randomly selected. Rather, they are integral elements of the Irish government's policy for primary and secondary education as stated in the White Paper on Education (1995). These are the expectations and requirements that we must bear in mind in discussions of teacher professionalism.

Implicit in our understanding of teacher professionalism is the specialist knowledge of teachers acquired after a prolonged period of training, the focus on the client/student as distinct from the pursuit of self-interest, a high degree of autonomy in their work, the ability to contribute to their own knowledge base and skills at both an individual and occupational level, and the fostering of student and community well-being. However, as Professor John Coolahan (1993) has noted, the most cursory examination of teachers' working lives "reminds of the historical contingency of professionalism in that the conditions or opportunities which exist may constrain or prevent the general exercise of professionalism". Thus, teachers in such countries as the United Kingdom, New Zealand, Canada and the United States have over the last two decades had to deal with very serious challenges to their professionalism. Such challenges have included changes in teacher education whereby it is de-professionalised and returned to an "apprenticeship model" of training which denies the need for expertise or a particular knowledge base; the imposition of bureaucratic burdens on teachers; the non-involvement of teachers and their representative organisations in the consultation process on education policy and, indeed, their displacement in this process by non-professionals.

Professionalism in teaching in very many developed and developing countries is not at all secure or taken for granted. The reasons for this are manifold but are perhaps best expressed as changes in the political structures in some States coupled with State commitment to the deregulation of all social institutions to ensure that they are more attuned to the requirements of the deregulated labour market and economy. Undermining the power of what are perceived as key interest groups such as the professions is part of that strategy of deregulation and change. Consequently, professionalism in teaching is a dynamic process in that it is contingent on circumstances in the broader socio-political arena and, as such, the argument for professionalism has to be made by each generation of teachers who have to be vigilant about their conditions of work and other aspects of their working lives which determine their professional status. Even where the status of teachers as professionals is well established as, for example, in the Republic of Ireland and in the Scandinavian countries, as a concomitant of that status teachers are increasingly expected by both the State and the public to be flexible and willing to take on the challenges outlined above and to be responsive to the requirements of our complex societies which are increasingly referred to as information societies. The challenge facing Irish teachers can be summarised as that of advancing the role and status of the teacher by creating a balance between public demands and the legitimate requirements of teachers that changes do not lead to a deterioration of their working conditions or erode their professional rights and responsibilities.

Teacher Professionalism in the Irish Context

As we look at teacher professionalism in the Irish context, we can take confidence from the very clear endorsement of the teaching profession that has emerged in the review of education policy in recent years. All of the official documents in this review have underlined the high quality of the teaching service and the high esteem in which it is held by the Irish public. A few quotes will affirm this:

> Ireland has been fortunate to maintain the quality of its teaching force (OECD, 1991).

> Teachers have made an enormous contribution to Irish
> society and it is important that the career of teaching
> continues to be an attractive and professionally reward-
> ing one (Department of Education, 1991).

> Views expressed at the Convention clearly indicated a
> high valuation of the professional and caring tradition of
> the Irish teaching force . . . concern was expressed that
> the status and profile of the teaching profession would
> be maintained (Department of Education, 1994).

> The quality, morale and status of the teaching profession
> are of central importance to the continuing development
> of a first-class education system in the decades ahead
> (Department of Education, 1995).

Aspects of Irish history and culture in part explain the high
regard for the work of teachers and their profession. However,
this is also inextricably linked to the work of the teacher unions which have over the years worked and fought long and
hard to secure proper conditions of employment for teachers,
opportunities for professional education and training and a role
for teachers in the education policy-making process. The current high degree of professionalisation in the Irish teaching
services is largely due to teachers themselves who have been
prepared to declare their professional status and take action to
defend that status.

The capacity of the teaching profession to organise was
noted by the 1991 OECD Review Team who referred to "the
very active and well organised professional teachers associations with their formidable negotiating skills". The teacher
unions at primary and post-primary level have a membership
of well over 90 per cent of those eligible. There is a strong
sense of cohesion and loyalty among the membership of the
unions. These characteristics have been demonstrated over the
years as teachers have sought to achieve key objectives concerning salaries and conditions of service. The unions have fos-

tered and continue to maintain broad-based support in Irish society, most notably within the wider trade union movement and, crucially, with parents' groups.

The exercise of the power by the teacher unions to achieve better conditions and salaries for teachers has contributed greatly to their status as professionals. Indeed, consolidating and improving the professional status of teachers is a key imperative for the teacher unions, as is evident from a selection of quotations from their constitutions and rules:

- The Constitution of the ASTI states that an objective of the Association is "to foster among members a sense of professional honour and esprit de corps".

- The Rule Book of the Teachers' Union of Ireland states that an objective of the Union is "to provide a means for the expression of the collective opinion of members on matters affecting their profession".

- The Constitution of the INTO states that an objective of the Organisation is to "promote the interests of education and to strive for the raising of educational standards".

Certainly, from the 1970s onwards, any dichotomy between the activities of the teacher unions to protect and defend their members' interests and to promote the professionalisation of the teaching force has disappeared. I should add that this trend is not confined to the teacher unions but, rather, in one way or another, has occurred in practically all trade unions, in particular the public sector unions. Indeed, the public sector unions have been to the forefront in defending their clients' interests in the face of Government cutbacks and regressive social policy. The ASTI, for example, was instrumental in highlighting the effects of education cutbacks in the 1980s on the quality of education available to children and on teachers' workloads and conditions. The advances which have taken place in the secondary education services in recent years are largely due to the tenacious pursuit by the ASTI of key objectives to reduce class size, improve funding for schools, expand programme choice for students, and increase opportunities for in-career training for teachers. In pursuing these objectives with the social partners, the ASTI is operating on the principle of creating a "virtuous circle" whereby well paid teachers working in well resourced schools with a broad and balanced curriculum can deliver the quality education service to young people which will enable them to cope with the changing labour market, the advent of the information society and the complex demands of citizenship as we approach the new millennium.

Challenges to Teacher Professionalism

The picture that I have painted thus far could give grounds for complacency in terms of the secure status of the teaching profession in modern Ireland. I would strongly caution against any resting on our laurels. As I emphasised earlier, teacher professionalism is a process rather than a given set of circumstances. Circumstances change and the teaching profession, which may be riding on the crest of a wave in one set of circumstances, may find itself battling to defend key values in another.

Today, serious challenges to teacher professionalism have emerged — some of which are related to broader social and economic changes and some of which are the result of political expediency. Central among the challenges are what I term the challenges of change. In this I include the pressures on schools to respond effectively, efficiently and, it would appear from some quarters, at minimal cost to the requirements of the economy, the changing labour market and to the broader changes in the social system. Public and, in particular, parental expectations of the education system also require schools to meet the needs — intellectual, educational, social and personal

— of all students. One has only to remind oneself of the frequency with which the term "multiple intelligences" is used to realise the profound nature of the changes that have taken place in the public consciousness concerning education. Consequently, on the agenda for change are curricular, pedagogic and assessment reform; the role of the school in providing supports for student welfare and guidance counselling; the role of the school to promote gender equality; the promotion of an enterprise culture and preparation for working life; the development of home-school-community relations.

Broadly speaking, the teaching profession has responded positively to these challenges. Indeed, teachers have in many instances been to the forefront in ensuring that changes have taken place in our schools to meet such challenges. The capacity of teachers to respond to these challenges will depend on the nature and level of resources — human and material — which are made available to schools. It will also critically depend on the opportunities for in-service training and professional development which are made available to teachers. The observation in the 1991 OECD Report that the "best returns from further investment in teacher education will come from the careful planning and construction of a nation-wide induction and in-service system using the concept of the teaching career as a foundation" is one which is widely shared by the teacher unions and is confirmed in the Education White Paper. The establishment of a Teaching Council, following enactment of the Teaching Council Bill, will, among other roles, serve to ensure the development of policy in the area of teacher education. Alongside strategic policy for teacher education, employment issues such as substitution, paid educational leave, secondment, job-sharing, additional remuneration and enhanced opportunities for promotion and career mobility must also be addressed. The absence of progress on these issues will serve as a disincentive to teachers' willingness to participate in in-career development.

The ASTI believes that structures to evaluate, assess and assist the operation of the education service are necessary. Such structures should be based on a "carrot rather than stick" philosophy and should aim to support and affirm the work of teachers in the school. In other words, the aim should be to assist teachers and schools in providing a quality education service rather than identifying and disciplining individual teachers. The model of inspection in the UK whereby school performance is monitored by non-professionals, individual teachers are appraised in a non-supportive manner and the performance of schools is publicised in simplistic league tables as part of a crude system of school funding based on a "payment by results" philosophy, is anathema to Irish teachers who are legitimately concerned that aspects of British OFSTED practice may intentionally or unintentionally be introduced into the Irish system. Ongoing consultation with the teaching profession must continue on evaluation structures which, in the final analysis, will have credibility only when they are developed in partnership and on the basis of consensus.

References

Coolahan, J. (1993), "Professionalism in Context" in Swan, D. and Leydon M. *Teachers as Professionals*, Dublin: ASTI/INTO/TUI, p. 8.

Department of Education (1991), *Green Paper on Education — Education for a Changing World*, Dublin.

Department of Education (1994), *Report of National Convention on Education*, Dublin, p. 85.

Department of Education (1995), *White Paper on Education: Charting our Education Future*, Dublin, p. 121.

Forfás (1996), *Shaping Our Future: A Strategy for Enterprise in Ireland in the 21st Century*, Dublin, p. 153.

OECD (1991), Review *of National Policy for Education: Ireland*, Paris: OECD, p. 100.

Robertson S.L. (1996), "Teachers' Work, Restructuring and Post-Fordism", in Hargreaves, A. and Goodson, F., *Teachers' Professional Lives*, London: Falmer Press, p. 29.

7

Catholic Church Influence in the Management of Second-Level Schools

Louis O'Flaherty

One of the more interesting developments in Irish education in the latter half of the twentieth century is the process by which the Catholic Church managed to extend its sphere of influence in second-level education at a time when the number of religious was declining and its moral authority was under criticism from an increasingly secularist society. The key to this apparent conundrum lies in the fact that the necessary steps to secure continuing control were undertaken before the revelations of clerical abuse which rocked public confidence in the 1990s.

At the beginning of the twentieth century the Catholic Church was still claiming an absolute right in educational matters. This claim was based on the literal interpretation of Christ's command "Teach ye all nations". The Church maintained that this mandate extended even to those who were non-Roman Catholic. This stance was re-stated in 1929 by Pope Pius XI in the encyclical *Divini Illius Magistri* (The Christian Education of Youth) and was eagerly accepted and promulgated by the Catholic Hierarchy in Ireland and taught as part of the Higher Diploma in Education courses in the constituent colleges of the National University until the late 1960s.

Apart from claiming an absolute right in the field of education, the Catholic Church in Ireland seemed to have had a particularly Jansenist attitude to co-education. Writing in 1932, the year of the Catholic Eucharistic Congress, the Rev Edward Cahill SJ, commenting on the aforementioned encyclical, said:

> Co-education which has wrought and is now wreaking such havoc in the United States and some other countries, and has become in its most extreme form one of the prominent characteristics of the new educational system of Russia, is gradually being introduced into Ireland in the last thirty years. It now obtains in University Colleges, some Technical Schools and to an extent even in Primary or National Schools (Cahill, 1932).

It can be noted that the one educational sector omitted from the above list was the secondary schools. In that sector separation of the sexes was almost total. When Fr Cahill published his views, he had done so secure in the knowledge that he was reflecting the views of the Catholic Bishops of Ireland who had held a special general meeting on 26 May 1926 and passed a resolution that "Mixed education in public schools is very undesirable, especially among the older children" (Concil. Plen. Maynut, 1929).

The two quotations given above can be seen as markers setting out criteria for vocational schools established under the Vocational Education Act, 1930. The comment from the bishops was in advance of the Act and Fr Cahill's book was published just as schools were being established under the terms of the Act. No one was to be in any doubt as to what should be the correct approach to the issue of co-education. At that time most of the secondary schools in the country were under the control of orders of teaching religious or diocesan clergy. There was a small number of Protestant secondary schools and a handful of schools run by lay Catholics but the vast majority of the 21,258 students who were enrolled in secondary schools in 1926 were in schools run by Catholic religious. This situation had come about as a direct result of the historical tensions which had existed between British authorities and the rights to Catholic education, going as far back as penal times.

The Catholic schools had been established and maintained by various Catholic agencies at a time when the state was unwilling to support those institutions. It might have been expected that the situation might change with the foundation of the new state. The Catholic authorities did not immediately change their attitude and the new State, for its part, was quite happy to live with the status quo as it was relieved of the problem of funding the secondary system. The private nature of the schools was recognised in the first annual report of the Department of Education (1925) when it said:

> The secondary system is largely a private one in which schools . . . retain their full autonomy in all matters of appointment and internal organisation.

Nearly 40 years later the Report of the Council of Education on the Curriculum of Secondary Schools set out what was perceived as the factual position of secondary schools at that time:

> First of all, they are strongly religious in character, religious motives having led to their foundation and religious bodies being, in the main, their trustees, patrons and managers. The dominant purpose of their existence is the inculcation of religious ideals and values (Council of Education, 1963).

The private nature of secondary schools has been recognised and accepted since the foundation of the State. At every point since then, when it was considered necessary to introduce new or alternative forms of second-level education, be they vocational, comprehensive or community schools and colleges, full prior consultation had to take place with religious authorities to ensure that they would not object to the proposed schools. In the environment which existed it would have been highly unlikely that such educational developments could have been successfully introduced without the tacit support of the Catholic hierarchy.[1]

Prior to the passing of the Vocational Education Act, 1930, guarantees were given to the Catholic hierarchy that the passing of the Act would not introduce a new principle of control in education and the Minister also tried to allay episcopal apprehensions about co-education under the Act (Coolahan, 1981). The courses to be given in the vocational schools would not be the same as those given in the traditional secondary schools. They were to be known as continuation courses and students would not be permitted to sit for the Intermediate or Leaving Certificate examinations. This privilege was to be reserved for the traditional secondary schools thus creating the impression that the vocational schools were somehow inferior to the longer established schools.

In the early 1960s only 30 per cent of the relevant cohort of Irish children was attending second-level schools. While this was a huge increase on the situation which had existed in 1926 when only 7 per cent were attending, it still fell short of what was deemed desirable. There were also pockets of extreme disadvantage within the country where participation rates were considerably lower than the national average. County Cavan had a participation rate of only 17.4 per cent, even though that had increased from a figure of 1 per cent in 1926 (Ó Buachalla, 1988).

It was because of these facts that Dr Paddy Hillery, Minister for Education in 1963, announced his intention to establish comprehensive schools "where facilities for post-primary edu-

---

[1] This issue is more fully developed in O'Flaherty (1992).

cation do not at present exist" (Hillery, 1963) He also made it very clear that he had had discussions with the Catholic hierarchy prior to his announcement:

> the vast majority or perhaps all of the pupils will be Catholics and having regard to the rights of parents, who in relation to the fundamental principles of education are represented by the Church's teaching authority, I have had consultation which is proceeding with the Catholic hierarchy on the management of these schools.

In the following years there was considerable debate as to the form and type of management structure which should be employed in the proposed new schools. Eventually it was agreed that a three-person board should be constituted to administer each school and that a nominee of the bishop in whose diocese the school was located should act as chairman.[2]

Despite the reference to the rights of parents in Dr Hillery's original statement, there was to be no representation for either parents or teachers on the boards of the new schools. This is the situation which continues to the present time despite numerous attempts by parent and teacher organisations to have the matter rectified. Another indication of the degree of control achieved by the Catholic hierarchy in the establishment of the new schools was the inclusion in the Articles of Management of a clause which reads:

> The Minister in consultation with the Bishop of the Diocese . . . may alter the terms of the scheme from time to time (Articles of Management for Comprehensive Schools, 1966).

---

[2] The three-person board comprised a nominee each of the Bishop, the VEC and the Minister. A subsequent development allowed for the establishment of five Protestant comprehensive schools where a five-person board structure included three nominees of the Protestant bishop.

In 1967 a scheme of free post-primary education was introduced in Ireland. This led to an unprecedented increase in the number of students wishing to attend. The O'Malley scheme, as it was popularly known, was seen not only as a political response to the celebration of the fiftieth anniversary of the 1916 rebellion but also as a recognition of the publication, in 1965, of the OECD Report, *Investment in Education*. This report is regarded by educationalists as being seminal in the development of educational policy in Ireland. The Autumn 1968 issue of *Studies* contained an article by Sean O'Connor who was then an assistant secretary in the Department of Education. The publication of this article was unprecedented as it was not the practice for civil servants to express publicly their views on matters pertaining to their professional areas of responsibility. In the article O'Connor made reference to the respective roles of Church and State in education. He postulated that in the changed atmosphere which was emerging, as a consequence of the introduction of free post-primary education, co-operation between secondary and vocational schools would be essential. He acknowledged the debt due to the Catholic Church in the provision of secondary education but he said that there should be dialogue between the Church and State on all the matters raised in his article. He wrote:

> No one wants to push the religious out of education: that
> would be disastrous, in my opinion. But I want them in
> as partners, not always as masters (O'Connor, 1968).

This rather innocuous comment drew down considerable criticism on O'Connor both from the Catholic school management organisations and the ASTI. In hindsight, the O'Connor article may be seen as the first shot in what was to become known as the community schools debate.

In October 1970 a document was sent from the Department of Education to the Catholic hierarchy outlining proposals for the establishment of community schools. There was a widespread feeling at that time that the schools which would evolve would be truly community-based and might be either multi-denominational or non-denominational and that the management structure should not be confined to any one religious group. This hope had been borne out of the experiences of the 1960s which had seen a great aspiration to ecumenism, as a consequence of the papacy of John XXIII and the civil rights movement, not to mention the problems which were emerging in Northern Ireland. Any hopes that may have been entertained about this happening were dispelled when Minister Padraig Faulkner (1970) stated in the Dáil:

> There is no question of interference by the State with school property. I wish to knock this idea on the head immediately. As explained the State will not be on the board of management of these schools or assume ownership in any form (Faulkner, 1970).

One interesting aspect of the community schools debate which was to drag on for most of the 1970s was that the Catholic Church seemed to have overcome its objections to co-education. A statement was issued by Cardinal Conway in 1972 in which he said that what he had hoped to see in Ardee, a town in his own diocese, was that the two Catholic schools should amalgamate to form a single Catholic co-educational school and that the vocational school should continue, whereas the Department of Education wanted all three to amalgamate. When Ballymun Comprehensive School had been built some years earlier, the two sexes had been kept separate at junior cycle. It was becoming evident that the critical factor in the provision of second-level education was not whether boys and girls should sit together in the same classroom so much as who should decide the philosophy and the ethos of the establishment.

In the case of community schools it became clear at a very early stage that the Catholic authorities were going to have a very direct input into their management.[3] There are currently 65 community schools in the country which have 10-person management boards representing religious authorities, the local VEC, parents and teachers. They also have the right to employ school chaplains paid for out of public funds, a right which has been upheld by the Supreme Court. While the schools are nominally multi-denominational they are essentially Roman Catholic in ethos and philosophy. The schools have made, and continue to make, a very valid contribution to Irish education.

By 1972, the changes in second-level education were beginning to cause concern to the Catholic hierarchy. The previous ten years had seen the introduction of free post-primary education and of two new types of school: comprehensive and community. In May 1972, a working party was established by the Catholic hierarchy to evaluate and report on the role of religious in education in Ireland in the coming decades. In February 1973, the working party presented its report entitled *The Future Involvement of Religious in Education*, which subsequently became known as the FIRE Report.

The FIRE Report confirmed what had already been suspected. The proportion of Catholic religious in religious-run secondary schools was in steady decline. In 1961/62, 57 per cent of the teachers in such schools were religious; in 1972/73 it was 34 per cent and the report indicated that that proportion was expected to drop to 28 per cent by 1975. This change was due to a number of factors, not least to the increased numbers attending secondary schools but also to the decline in vocations and the ageing of those religious who were already in education. It was obvious from the Report that a new situation was beginning to emerge where it would no longer be possible to

---

[3] For a more detailed account of their development, see O'Flaherty (1992).

run schools if they were to be staffed by a high proportion of religious. This Report suggested six possible courses of action for the future and one of these was "to share management of religious schools with lay people" (Education Commission of Major Religious Superiors and the Hierarchy, 1973). This proposal may not seem particularly innovative when viewed from 1999 but at the time it was quite revolutionary.

Religious-run secondary schools had been established in Ireland as institutions separate and distinct from the State. To the ordinary citizen they were owned and administered by the priests, brothers and nuns. Sometimes they employed lay teachers but neither they nor the parents of the children who attended the schools had ever been permitted to participate in the administration or governance of the institutions. They were run by people who had a very definite religious mission and were prepared to undertake the task for very little monetary reward either from the State or society in general. They did not tolerate interference in that mission. Society accepted that position, as can be substantiated by reference to numerous ministerial and public statements on the role of religious in education. The proposals in the FIRE report were revolutionary insofar as the religious were prepared to compromise on new forms of management if:

> it could conceivably be the means of ensuring continuity
> of Catholic education in the hands of lay teachers should
> the religious withdraw from a school. (Ibid.)

As a result of the implementation of the proposals in the FIRE Report, devolved management structures have been introduced into more than 80 per cent of religious or clerically-owned Catholic secondary schools while the proportion of religious who are teaching in these schools has dropped to 5 per cent. The result has been that many of the schools have effectively become lay Catholic schools with lay principals. With the current drop in religious vocations it is unlikely that there will be any direct involvement of religious in these schools in the near future.

While the Catholic religious authorities were consolidating and expanding their own schools, they also managed to extend their sphere of influence into the vocational sector. They have participated in the establishment of community colleges where they have a direct input into the governance of what are essentially vocational schools. There are now 36 such schools in the State. All of the developments since the early 1960s have helped to expand the sphere of Catholic education at second level, and for the most part it must be said that this move has been generally welcomed by the public.

The problem which has begun to emerge, and which will become even more apparent in the future, hinges on the very success of the expansionary nature of Catholic influence in second-level education in the past 35 years. Catholic schools in Ireland were originally established not only for missionary purposes but also to help those on the margins of a colonial society. They could have been seen as socially radical insofar as they were opposed to the social system that existed in the eighteenth and nineteenth centuries. They are now very much part of the established order, a fact which has been acknowledged by the Conference of Religious in Ireland (CORI, 1997).

There is evidence to suggest that the greater the religious involvement in second-level schools, the higher will be the participation rates of the middle to upper-middle classes in such schools. This is happening at a time in Ireland when actual religious practice is in decline and there is little evidence to suggest that religious practice is higher among the members of higher socio-economic groupings. As one commentator has said:

> The building of a local Christian community has clearly not been an objective of most Catholic secondary schools. Indeed, the local social class and ability divisions amongst pupils and parents in most multi-school catch-

ment areas not only reinforces, but even aggravates, local class/status hierarchies (Hannan, 1997).

This is particularly evident in the small number of fee-paying secondary schools, most of which are under some form of Catholic clerical management. Few of these schools have any devolved management structure. They enjoy a particular privilege in Ireland, as, unlike the situation which obtains in other countries, the State continues to pay a very high proportion of the teachers' salaries. In these instances the presence of religious can appear to reinforce social divisions. This perception has been the cause of concern for some religious involved in education and has been a factor in their seeking alternative roles for their vocations.

The problem for the future may revolve around the very ethos of the second-level school system. It is generally accepted that the ethos of a school is formed by the beliefs and attitudes of the students, parents, teachers and management. Whatever constants that existed and were shared by these groups in the past would seem to be under threat. In the changed circumstances will the Catholic influence continue to be central to these schools, or will their values and attitudes change, as they did in relation to co-education, in order to maintain control in changed times?

In the past the Catholic Church has been reluctant to accept the concept of civic or social morality. In the recent past this was evident in the debate on divorce and other secular issues. There has been a tendency to regard the State as something second-best. Yet structure and order are essential for the continuance of a civilised society. The role of the Catholic Church has been widespread and central in Irish education. It is difficult to see how such a dominant role can be maintained in the future without surrendering some of those values which the Church would regard as immutable. The question which must inevitably be asked is, will the Church be forced to withdraw from those schools in which it invested so much and will all the efforts of the past 35 years to expand its field of influence in education be set at nought, not by a State takeover as was feared, but rather by a realisation that the institutional Church may be out of synch with the wishes and aspirations of the very parents whom it had educated?

References

Articles of Management for Comprehensive Schools (1966).

Cahill, Edward (1932), *The Framework of a Christian State*, Dublin: M.H. Gill & Son, p. 374

Concil. Plen. Maynut 1927 (1929), *Acta et Decreta*, Appendix, p. 19.

Coolahan, John (1981), *Irish Education: History and Structure*, Dublin: IPA, p. 98.

CORI Education Commission (1997), *Religious Congregations in Irish Education: A Role in the Future*, Dublin: CORI.

Council of Education (1963), *The Curriculum of the Secondary School*, Dublin: The Stationery Office.

Department of Education (1925), Report, pp. 7–8.

Education Commission of Major Religious Superiors and the Hierarchy (1973), *The Future Involvement of Religious in Education*, report of a working party submitted to the Chairman, February.

Faulkner, P. (1970), *Dáil Reports*, Vol. 249, 19 November, Col. 1616.

Hannan, Damien (ed.) (1997), *The Future of Trusteeship: A Review of Some Options for the Way Forward*, Dublin: CORI, p. 25.

Hillery, Dr P.J. (1963), Minister for Education, statement at press conference, 20 May.

Ó Buachalla, Seamus (1988), *Education Policy in Twentieth Century Ireland*, Dublin: Wolfhound Press, p. 384.

O'Connor, S. (1968), *Studies*, Vol. LVII, Autumn, No. 227, p. 249.

O'Flaherty, Louis (1992), *Management and Control in Irish Education: The Post-Primary Experience*, Dublin: Drumcondra Teachers' Centre, p. 7.

8

Attempts to Tackle Disadvantage — Blitzkrieg or Phoney War? (A Second-Level Perspective)

Tony Deffely

A Chip on His Shoulder?

Noel N. Other is 15 years old. Three years ago, his father, John, an unemployed man, died of a heart attack. Noel's two elder brothers left school last year having completed a basic Junior Certificate. He has no interest in school, dodges class when he can and doesn't bring his books home, preferring to leave them in his school locker. Noel is well known to the Gardaí and often puts up one or two fingers when the squad car passes. He doesn't show much ability. He's a poor reader and teachers complain that he has a millisecond attention span. He's probably smoking hash or grass and is seen drunk at discos.

The family live on a fairly basic local authority housing scheme and Noel and his mates rule the roost. Some teachers will privately admit to being afraid of them and hate to meet them outside school because of catcalls and insulting remarks. Noel's mother has begun another relationship and will not come to the school when requested.

This year Noel will complete his Junior Certificate and tells everyone that he's leaving school then.

Some teachers relate well to Noel in that he will bid them the time of day. But many will suggest that his presence in class is depriving other pupils of a decent chance to learn. He shouts, walks around at will and the teachers' efforts to control him are time-consuming, break up the flow of the teaching and put everyone in a giddy and ugly mood. If Noel can be nursed through the Junior Certificate many will feel that it's a great achievement.

Noel has a chip on his shoulder. Somewhere along the line he's picked up the idea that the system was against him from the start and that things are not going to get any better. The fingers for the squad car may be a metaphor.

In fact, Noel will not be an isolated stastistic. The 1995 OECD Economic Survey of Ireland showed that 31 per cent of children from a manual unskilled background completed junior cycle only, while the corresponding figure for those from a higher professional background was 2.9 per cent. Some 52.9 per cent of students from a higher professional background gained five or more honours at Leaving Certificate level compared with 4.1 per cent from an unskilled background. Noel's early trips to the local ICTU centre for the unemployed with his mother might have enabled him to pick up a message — if he was interested. From the date that fate selected his family background his chances were poor.

What are We Doing?

The White Paper on Education, *Charting Our Education Future* (1995), sets out targets for completion of second level.

> A major objective will be that the percentage of the six-teen-to-eighteen-year-old agegroup completing senior cycle will increase to at least 90 per cent by the year 2000 (p. 44).

In recent years, a number of schemes have been initiated by the Department of Education and Science to help schools in combating disadvantage at second level. They have sought to allocate resources in the following ways.

Disadvantaged Posts

Additional posts have been given to 190 second-level schools which have been judged to be disadvantaged. Personally, at second level, I believe that there is a need to seriously analyse what is happening in relation to the additional posts for the disadvantaged. At the risk of being cast out by the great family of teachers for disloyalty and inaccuracy, I would suggest that not many of those posts exist in terms of clear identifiability. I would suggest that there are few staff rooms that one could go into and find such a teacher with a specific programme to deal with that brief. Instead, one would find that the hours are spread across the timetable in order to fill gaps in curricula.

I have often argued, and often in vain, that that is not the best way to use that resource. I believe that a "real life" as opposed to hypothetical teacher for the disadvantaged would produce a much greater impact in a school both as identifiable advocate and developer of programmes.

The suggestion that these posts were used to solve the staffing problems of management rather than the real problems of disadvantage is demoralising and would be vehemently denied by some.

I believe that the real-life teacher with real-life commitment in staff-meetings, in the unions, in relating to school management, in creating pressure other than points pressure, in the development of best practice, in attendance at specific in-service training, in the development and analysis of programmes, in relating with home/school liaison, in terms of team leadership and of overall advocacy, could have real impact.

The generalised use of the disadvantaged post has deprived the disadvantaged of a voice.

Home/School/Community Liaison Teachers

There are 84 out of a total of 762 second-level schools which can avail of the Home/School/Community Liaison Scheme focusing on disadvantaged areas. Only schools whose main feeder schools are eligible for the liaison scheme can currently avail of this service. Schools catering for disadvantage across a wider catchment area incorporating ineligible primary schools cannot make application for such a post. Within the scheme, home/school liaison teachers work with parents to develop positive involvement in their children's education and build towards having good relations between the parents and the school.

The Home/School/Community Liaison Scheme is an excellent idea but is marred by the fact that liaison teachers are not entitled to hold that position and a promoted post in the school simultaneously. It certainly does nothing for morale.

Extra Capitation

Secondary schools eligible for a disadvantaged post get an extra £30.00 per pupil. In the case of Community/Comprehensive and VEC schools the overall grant is raised to allow for this additional amount. I do not know if specific returns are made in relation to the utilisation of that money.

Remedial Teachers

A total of 350 ex-quota remedial posts are allocated, in addition to 147 resource posts, to serve the 762 second-level schools which serve the 370,000 pupils at this level of education — slightly more than one per thousand.

The allocation of a remedial post is at the discretion of the Department and there is no automatic eligibility.

Tracking

A pilot initiative is in place, since February 1998, to develop policies to tackle early school leaving. This will involve tracking pupils to ensure that they do not drift out of the system unnoticed. It will in time provide some interesting insights. However, it's a pity that, with all the crocodile tears, conferences and papers over the years, no specific research is available outside of the School Leavers Survey about what is happening to children like Noel who drop out early. An Oireachtas committee is currently examining the situation and it is hoped that they will shine some light on the subject.

Other Initiatives

Although it is not the focus of this chapter, initiatives at primary level will have a huge impact on second level where levels of literacy and numeracy can be used as a rough predictor of subsequent school performance.

Compensatory education is also in place for young people outside the education system, notably Junior Education Centres for Travellers between 15 and 18 years old and senior Travellers' centres offering combined education, work experience and training to Travellers between 16 and 25 years old.

Youthreach centres provide basic skills training up to NCVA Foundation Level, Junior Certificate, and NCVA Level 1, and pay basic rates to early school leavers from 15 to 18 years old. They serve early school leavers well and significantly benefit young people's lives.

Despite the regulation that an aspiring trainee must be six months out of school before entering the scheme, many principals are delighted to "place" particular students there in order to get them off their hands.

In other words — that which was there to reconnect them with the system is that which disconnects them from it. But it is unwise to complain lest the much-valued "way to get rid of a troublesome student" should be denied.

Perhaps the necessity to have viable numbers may also serve as a spur in the recruitment of school students as trainees. Some trainees are actually accepted after they have completed their Junior Certificate. One can only pity a principal who is approached by a parent and pupil for a letter to go to Youthreach. They don't have the resources to cater for the needs of the pupil and are forced to see them go to a well-resourced Centre where the objective is to send them back to school. How that principal must wish their school had been given sufficient resources to begin with.

An Elementary Junior Certificate has been put in place to assist less-able students to achieve in a positive way.

Guidance counsellors provide guidance in schools and help students grow in self-knowledge and self-esteem. Figures from the *Guidelines for the Practice of Guidance and Counselling in Schools* (1996) show 331 out of 762 second-level schools entitled to a guidance counsellor on an ex quota basis of 500–1. Another 266 are entitled to half a guidance counsellor while other schools are entitled to even less. In the 1980s this ratio was set at 250–1. It is extraordinary that the cut in guidance should continue to be implemented in a key area to do with disadvantage while at the same time official policy is professing to be concerned about the issue.

A pastoral care system operates in many schools whereby a particular teacher takes particular responsibility for a class group and nurtures them during their time in the school.

A psychological service is currently provided to second-level schools with just 20 psychologists servicing 768 schools and 370,000 students. Plans are being discussed to considerably reduce this ratio.

Community Groups Pilot Initiatives

In addition to Department initiatives, Area Development Management (ADM) through Sub Programmes II of the Local Urban and Rural Development Programme also seeks to counter disadvantage through support for committed communities. These initiatives have taken many forms through programmes which have been accepted for funding. In addition to programmes for those at risk of leaving school, they include:

- Programmes to prevent under-achievement

- Programmes to provide support for specific target groups

- Programmes to address specific disadvantage

- Developmental Programmes.

Analysis of the success of these is limited but it is to be hoped that implementable programmes will emerge from this funded process which will prove beneficial to the disadvantaged.

Initiatives at local level include:

- After school projects aimed at helping potential early school leavers to develop social, interpersonal and communication skills;

- Homework clubs aimed at encouraging the development of good study skills in a supportive homework environment;

- Transition programmes aimed at easing transition from primary to second level;

- Literacy and numeracy interventions;

- Initiatives with parents;

- Matching and mentoring initiatives in which young people are matched with adults who would seek to advise and mentor them;

- School/Community links for support and activities;

- Targeting specific groups — young people with disabilities; Travellers etc.;

- Third-level access programmes.

Apprentices

Under the auspices of FÁS, applicants may accept an apprenticeship at 16 years of age. This sets a real and psychological benchmark for those thinking of leaving school early. The decision to leave after Junior Certificate for an apprenticeship provides a model for those who may not be interested in being an apprentice but who are nevertheless unsettled.

It seems odd that, despite the new Ministerial suggestions in relation to continuing education for early school leavers, the apprenticeship entry age and qualification standard remains so low — 16 years old with five subjects in the Junior Certificate. How can a system that aspires to keep young people in school to Leaving Certificate level simultaneously tempt them to leave?

Certainly it appears even more strange when a student who completes their Leaving Certificate in subjects like technical graphics, construction studies, engineering or the Leaving Certificate Applied must serve exactly the same apprenticeship as the early school leaver with a Junior Certifictate or pre-apprenticeship course. This apprenticeship entry-level benchmark is not a good idea. It also serves to weaken the ladder to technician level and higher education and provides a veneer of respectability for early school leaving.

Others are tempted to leave school for poorly-regulated traineeships such as hairdressing or butchery. Proper regulation would provide the spur to continue in education.

So — What's Up Doc?

Despite positive approaches and the White Paper's ambitious aspirational completion rates of 90 per cent, real completion percentages for Leaving Certificate sit in the low-80s. Somewhere, something is wrong, as the old Chinese wall posters used to say. At a time of unprecedented growth at third level and wealth in society do we have the commitment to put it right?

Some would argue that educational development always results from the needs of the economy and never from the needs of the people. If there is a compelling argument to deal with disadvantage then it will be an economic one.

Those arguments will focus on the costs of failing to resolve the problems of disadvantaged children in relation to the type of adults they will become. The future financial costs of their inability to function as independent economic and social units and the loss of the potential consequent benefits to themselves and to all society will be of primary concern.

This may seem to disregard the idea of equality for all but if the devil must quote scripture to his own ends, then so be it.

You May Say I'm a Dreamer!

Perhaps we should also consider the entire question in material terms.

Perhaps an argument should be made that teachers working with the disadvantaged-quota classes should draw special lucrative allowances and have special training and qualifications.

In a flat profession the development of a pedagogic promotion as opposed to an administrative one might prove popular. Teachers working with disadvantaged students could be assisted by strong support systems in both teaching and personal terms to avoid the real possibility of burnout. They should be assured of a return to a more standard setting when and if they wished, with the special allowance counting towards pension.

The suggestion has often been made that what is currently happening in some schools is in fact the opposite. In some schools weaker classes are identified as places where a less functional teacher is placed to do as little damage as possible to the "good classes" and, ultimately, to enrolment. In other cases they may be used as a "sin bin" for those staff members who are judged inadequate or who have erred in the eyes of management. Many parents, too, resent having their child "held back" by students with difficulties, be they disadvantaged or otherwise.

Schools in competitive situations which insist on mixed ability classes may find themselves "punished come enrolment day" by ambitious parents. The ruthlessness of parents' ambitions for their children and their disregard for the societal consequences of elitist schools — even among the most socially progressive — often astounds me.

Unless schools are careful they can rapidly become ghettos for the disadvantaged with nothing to show except demoralisation and marginalisation. It's much easier to expel or exclude, with of course, the additional benefit of underlining the need for strict discipline among the remainder.

That young person can then toddle along to another school with a reputation for taking such pupils but no additional resources. Alternatively, they can drop out.

Imagine a system where only the best and really gifted teachers could teach the disadvantaged quota mixed ability classes with special hefty allowances. Imagine if significant additional staffing and class oriented grants and allowances were targeted at schools with the necessary enrolment and where serious monitoring ensured that there was no hiving off.

Imagine a situation where having a child in a mixed ability class with a disadvantaged quota would enable them to benefit from the enriched teaching services available. The arguments for streaming might come under attack.

Let us imagine that teaching the disadvantaged had the same requirements in terms of special qualifications and salary advantages as lecturing at third level. (Sadly, recent paltry pay awards in Youthreach suggest that my vision for this area is more fantasy than hallucination.)

Let us imagine that retaining pupils' interest and attendance at school was market driven in terms of the retention of those same allowances for staff and school. Suddenly, in addition to the professional interest of teachers, the continued enrolment of each pupil would be of value in financial terms. That student would then have value and be in special care within the school system.

The intrinsic reward would be their presence, rather than their absence. In some cases now, whether we like it or not, the ultimate hidden reward for school, teachers, other pupils and their parents may be the departure of a troubled student from the school.

Imagine, even, a situation where every pupil arriving in second level came complete with a comprehensive dossier. This could provide the basis for discussion at a formal interface between second and primary level with serious objective-setting to include parents, Home/School/Community Liaison, School Attendance Officer, teacher for the disadvantaged, etc., and the Social Services, if necessary.

For Noel the Junior Certificate is looming closer. He roams the corridor like a stray. He holds office in the toilets and stinks of cigarettes. His attendance is getting worse. He's lost his part-time job in the coleslaw wholesalers for hygiene reasons. Even the Leaving Certificate students have begun to mutter about why he's kept in school. Noel is on the edge. Perhaps that's where he'll always be, unless there's a war.

9

Further Education: Challenge and Opportunity

Jim Dorney

One of the most important developments in Irish education in recent years, and one of the most far-reaching in its implications, has been the growth of further education (FE). Over 20,000 students in second-level schools are currently enrolled on post-Leaving Certificate courses certified by the National Council for Vocational Awards (NCVA), together with smaller numbers of students taking courses certified by agencies such as BTEC, City and Guilds and some UK universities. The Teachers' Union of Ireland (TUI) welcomes the growth and development of the FE sector, since it greatly increases the range of educational opportunities available and can be seen as consistent with the tradition established by the 1930 Vocational Education Act. However, the union also recognises the challenges and difficulties that have arisen from largely unplanned and uncoordinated growth in this area. Some of these challenges include:

- The difficulty of defining further education
- The status and conditions of teachers on such courses
- The regulation of provision in the FE area

- Continuity and progression

- The role of the National Qualifications Authority.

Each of these issues will be considered in turn.

Defining Further Education

The difficulty of defining further education lies in the diversity of provision in this sector, in the diversity of locations in which further education is provided and the range of educational levels of the courses included in its remit. Unlike other European countries, including the UK, the leaders of development in the FE area in Ireland have been in the education sector. The development of FE in vocational schools has been consistent with the requirements of the 1930 Act, but has updated and extended the concepts of "continuation" and "technical", as used in the Act. "Continuation" education in 1930 began at age 14 for those students who, in the words of Memo V40, had to "start early in life", and who were thus excluded from mainstream academic educational provision. The brief of vocational education was to prepare them for "the occupations which are open to them". This was clearly seen as a limited range of options and "continuation" education was explicitly separated from "general" education by the assurances famously given by the then Minister for Education, John Marcus O'Sullivan, to the Irish Catholic bishops.

The 1930 Act defined "technical education" as:

> education pertaining to trades, manufactures, commerce and other industrial pursuits (including the occupations of girls and women connected with the household) and in subjects bearing thereon and relating thereto, and includes education in science, art, music, and physical training.

"Technical" education still includes education pertaining to trades, in the traditional sense of the term, and the traditional practical subjects, including those in the secretarial area, still hold a justly honoured place in Irish vocational schools. TUI has long played a leading role in articulating the continued curricular importance of genuine practical subjects which engage students in real problem-solving with real materials. The justification for these technical subjects is essentially a liberal one, based on the development of skill and creativity of students, rather than on the needs of employers or of that mythical beast, the "economy". Mike Cooley, in *Architect or Bee?*, points out the social implications and, especially, the risks for trade unionists, in the separation of intellectual work from manual work, in the introduction of neo-Taylorist views and the de-humanisation of the workplace. The development of FE in an educational setting can help to prevent a purely instrumentalist and reactive approach to the development of vocationally-relevant courses.

"Technical" now embraces a very wide range of technologies and activities and it is estimated that 60 per cent of the technology that we will be using in 10 years' time has yet to be invented. Vocational courses thus have to prepare people to be flexible and to be able to continue learning throughout their lives. "Flexibility" has become a term dreaded and rejected by trade unionists because unscrupulous employers have defined it narrowly to mean a willingness to accept low wages and infinitely extendable working hours. Genuine flexibility would include scope and reward for workers' creativity and a negotiated organisation of work in a way that is mutually beneficial to workers and employers. FE courses must therefore encourage the development of creativity, originality, self-esteem and thinking skills in the same manner as all other worthwhile educational courses. This type of course can also contribute to economic development in that it can anticipate, rather than merely react to, technological trends and opportunities. An example can be found in the development of courses in the area of the music industry and in film animation which have actually allowed the creation of new types of employment in an Irish context.

Further education includes not only post-Leaving Certificate courses, but also apprenticeship and workplace training, as well as compensatory programmes, such as Youthreach. What these courses have in common is that they are outside what has come to be regarded as the standard educational route: primary education to secondary education to third level to employment. They have a vocational dimension and they make particular demands on teachers, over and above those made by "normal" educational courses. It is these demands that are considered in the next section.

Status and Conditions of Teachers

Flexibility in course design has obvious benefits for participants and for future employers. It is, however, very demanding on the teachers who design, deliver and assess these courses. TUI, as the union representing most of the teachers involved in FE, makes no apology for continuing to demand appropriate recognition for the level of courses in which these teachers are engaged and for the necessary supports to be put in place to enable the courses to be developed to their full potential and thus meet very important needs for participants and for the economy. For those courses for which the entry level is Leaving Certificate, the appropriate level is clearly that already defined in national agreements, i.e. third-level lecturing structures. It is clear that the nature of the work differs radically from second-level teaching, not just in content, but in the requirement that teachers are involved in ongoing development, administration and marketing of courses. The shortness of the cycle in one-year courses makes its own particular kinds of demands on teachers. Barely has one cohort embarked on a course when the modules for the next session have to be planned and teachers have to be actively involved in seeking next year's students.

The success of post-Leaving Certificate courses is all the more remarkable when it is borne in mind that many have been delivered in second-level classrooms and require considerable teacher ingenuity to overcome the lack of purpose-designed textbooks, third level standard equipment and technician support. All of these issues need to be addressed together with the provision of in-service training and opportunities for teachers to spend periods of time in industry in order to develop their awareness of labour market trends.

It is clear that the availability of FE courses has contributed significantly to education and to economic development, but the sector's very growth and success brings with it the need for appropriate forms of regulation so that student needs and not market forces are of primary concern.

Regulation of Provision

The case was set out above for the recognition of educational settings as the primary area for course development in the FE area. Such an approach allows for maximum flexibility in the choice of course content and allows the student-focused, personal development approach to continue. TUI is concerned that market forces should not become the main regulators of provision in the FE area, since this militates against a needs-based approach. The recent legislation, the Qualifications (Education and Training) Act (1999) causes some concern in this regard, since the section on course validation implies that a multiplicity of providers, many of them commercial, is envisaged. The track record of public sector schools in this area must be taken into account and destructive competition between providers must be avoided. The vocational nature of FE courses must not be allowed to obscure their public service dimension and their role in contributing to equality of educational opportunity. TUI has called for the setting up of a Further Education Authority, separate from the certifying body, which would have the role of engaging in ongoing course development, in the provision of in-service support to teachers and in the regulation of competition between providers. Regulation of provision is also important in the context of ensuring continuity and progression between courses.

Continuity and Progression

If FE is to contribute significantly to the extension of educational opportunities, courses must be designed so that they lead to continuing educational opportunities as well as to employment. This puts an extra demand on course design and development. It is surely in an educational setting that educational continuity can best be fostered. Within this setting, existing links can be strengthened and ladders of progression developed. This is particularly important for students who have participated in FE courses as adult returners (e.g. through VTOS dispersed mode) and who wish to have the option of continued participation in the education system. It is disappointing in this regard that recognition of level-three courses has been so slow and it is difficult to escape the conclusion that deliberate delaying tactics are being used by the Department of Education and Science to frustrate the TUI claim for third level recognition. The case for continuity and progression must be considered on its own merits, independently of other non-educational considerations.

The legislation to set up the National Qualifications Authority is, therefore, to be welcomed.

The National Qualifications Authority

The legislation for the National Qualifications Authority was preceded by the work of TEASTAS on whose Board the late Michael Enright served with distinction. The terms of the Act will influence the development of the further education sector through the establishment of a Further Education and Training Awards Council. The legislation throws down challenges to TUI regarding a number of issues, including:

- **The continued development of Further Education courses.** The primary role of the proposed Further Education and Training Council is accreditation and validation of courses in further education. There continues to be an ongoing need for facilitation of the development of new courses.

- **The future role of the Institutes of Technology will be influenced by the NQA.** The proposed dissolution of the NCEA presents new challenges to the Institutes of Technology, as does dissolution of NCVA to further education. TUI sees it as vital that schools are supported in the complex task of developing, delivering and assessing further education courses.

- **The balance between public and private sector involvement.** TUI believes that education is a public service and that FE is an important dimension of this provision.

- **The regulation of provision in the FE area.** TUI believes that destructive competition between providers of FE should be avoided and the legislation makes no recommendation in this regard.

- **The proposed arrangements for quality assurance.**
  Arrangements for quality assurance must be developed by
  negotiation and agreement.

All of these challenges will be taken on by TUI and we look
forward to lively debate and to fruitful negotiations on these
issues. The further education sector represents an area of
growth, challenge, debate and, ultimately, extension of educational opportunity. TUI will engage whole-heartedly in the discussion process to bring about progress in this area.

Michael Enright had a real commitment to the disadvantaged in society; second chance education was an issue about
which he felt strongly. We hope that the development of the
further education sector will meet the aspirations which he had
to allow people who missed out in formal education to have a
second chance.

10

From Clockwork to Porridge: Is There "One Right Way" to Manage Schools?

Gearóid Ó Brádaigh

Introduction

David Hume, writing in the middle part of the eighteenth century, made the following poignant observation:

> All inferences from experience suppose, as their foundation, that the future will resemble the past and that similar powers will be conjoined with similar sensible qualities. If there be any suspicion that the course of nature may change, and that the past may be no rule for the future, all experience becomes useless and can give rise to no inference or conclusion. It is impossible, therefore, that any arguments from experience can prove this resemblance of the past to the future, since all these arguments are founded on the supposition of that resemblance (Hume, 1748, p. 51).

In what was then an age of mechanistic rationalism it would seem that Hume's opinion must have been a minority view of the world. In the context of the post-modern maxim, "don't trust anything", Hume was certainly ahead of his time. Scientific developments in this century have indicated that the view of the world as expressed by David Hume was a good deal more accurate than many would have given him credit for at the time.

It is a fact that for many people in the modern and post-modern eras our view of the world has been, for the most part, informed by a mechanistic, reductionist, rationalist interpretation of the world around us and it is this view which has permeated most of our personal, institutional and social interactions. In particular, it is a world view which has helped shape our theories of management in business and our philosophy in education. For a growing number of people it has been both refreshing and disturbing to realise that this Enlightenment view of the world is not the whole picture or even half of it. There is an alternative world view — much more akin to Hume's — which suggests that our universe is not clock-like, not a giant algorithm moving from cause to effect, not predictable and not reducable to molecular parts each of which can be examined under the microscope and reassembled; rather our universe is a wholeness of interconnected parts which move in random patterns from order to disorder, from equilibrium to chaos, in a manner which is not predictable in the traditional sense. It is a web of relationships, "a porridge of being", (Wheatley, 1992, p. 141), a universe where chaos reigns.

Clockwork: Conventional Management

The Age of Enlightenment heralded a new age in science, human thinking and government. Enlightenment thinkers sought to base all knowledge in science, to establish a new epistemology based on an encyclopaedic knowledge. The growth in scientific knowledge and the consequent developments in economic theory and methods of production had enormous implications for society. Analytical philosophy, particularly that set out by Descartes, emphasised rationalism in scientific investigation. Descartes imagined the world as one huge clockwork that moved with both precision and stability. The cornerstone of the rationalist view of the world is that we can understand the universe by analysing the various causes and effects which manifest themselves within it and, through a process of reason based on the precision and stability of the universe, predict future courses of action and events.

As western society moved from the Age of Enlightenment to the Industrial Age, with its concomitant growth in bourgeois structures, production processes expanded to make use of an increasingly more complex and technically more sophisticated culture. By the modern age, labour and management had become more subdivided, quantifiable and measurable and less autonomous and reflective.[1] Applying this paradigm to the context of organisational theory, many commentators (Capra, 1983; Wheatley, 1992; Stacey, 1991; and Cavaleri, 1993) hold the view that it is immediately obvious that many of the underlying principles of rationalist/analytical philosophy have been applied to what they describe as conventional management. According to Stacey it is "conventional" in two ways: most managers profess to be aiming toward it and most textbooks reinforce it (Stacey, 1993, p. 13). The proposition put forward is that the most prominent and readily acceptable models of management have all imported their methodology from traditional science and, with that, they have imported the machine-like frame of reference within which traditional science explains how the world works. In this focus we view organisations as groups of people with a common purpose, striving towards status quo or equilibrium. Where change is encountered or required it is approached from a systematic point of view which suggests that change can and must be predicted and controlled in a manner which absorbs the change and restores equilibrium. In this paradigm managing an organisation consists of gathering detailed data from the external environment and, having devised an appropriate algorithm, making predictions about future events and adjusting accordingly. For example, planning is essentially regarded as making decisions in the present about events in the future. For the most part, this method of organisational control is based on the assumption that most, if not all, of the relevant data is available for scrutiny. This assumption will be examined in more detail below.

Cavaleri and Obloj (1993) describe this as a "hard-systems" approach to management. They hold the view that in certain circumstances (e.g. well-defined production or operational problems) it does hold the key to the development of economical solutions. It is not difficult to envisage many aspects of organisational/production management where such an approach could be very useful. In common with classical science, hard-systems theory is reductionist in character; in both cases greater understanding, greater control, is secured through breaking the whole into smaller parts for detailed study. But just as theories in classical science cannot deal with the myriad phenomena presented to it, so too rational, hard-systems models of management fail to deal with all organisational phenomena. For example, where common goals are not shared, where conflicting opinions and different preferences apply within an organisation, where uncertainty reigns and the future cannot be agreed upon, rational management tends to compensate by introducing strictly hierarchical methods of control and supervision. This has serious implications for the leadership style within the organisation and these are examined below.

Porridge: New Science and New Management

Scientific developments in the closing decades of the last century and the early decades of this century led scientists to the observation that the universe does not always behave in the ordered manner set down by traditional interpretations. Building on this discovery, science developed the theories of relativity and quantum mechanics which showed that, contrary to traditional belief, matter can behave in a random, apparently haphazard fashion which does not derive from a strictly linear cause-effect relationship. The universe is not striving towards equilibrium but is in a constant state of change. Depending on the precise nature of this change, matter will either develop by small incremental changes or will become transformed into an entirely new existence. This movement is not always predictable but is "chaotic" in a particular sense of that term. Chaos does not mean complete disorder but a response to a complex range of feedback loops that, in turn, create new emissions or responses. Stacey defines "chaos" as:

> An inherently random pattern of behaviour generated by fixed inputs into deterministic (that is fixed) rules (relationship), taking the form of non-linear feedback loops. Although the specific path followed by the behaviour so generated is random and hence unpredictable in the long-term, it always has an underlying pattern to it. A "hidden" pattern, a global pattern or rhythm. That pattern is self-similarity, that is a constant degree of variation, consistent variability, regular irregularity or more precisely, a constant fractal dimension. Chaos is therefore order (a pattern) within disorder (random behaviour) (Stacey, 1993, p. 228).

It is in this context that we can see more clearly the profound importance of Hume's remarks as quoted above; for although he wrote this piece more than two centuries ago, it was not until the middle of this century that scientists fully realised that the future is not predictable and that the organisation of the universe is not something that can be controlled by the laws of traditional physics. It is the universe that determines the parts and not the other way around.

In the area of philosophy, this century saw the development of epistemologies which challenge the more traditional notions of causality. The work of Wittgenstein in conjunction with the work carried out by the Frankfurt School (especially that of Theodor Adorno) challenged the distinction between "observation" and "interpretation". This work set aside the traditional distinctions between analytic and empirical philosophy, between theory and practice, object and subject, fact and value. It put forward the proposition that how any social situation is defined will depend on a synthesis of observation and interpretation and this, in turn, will depend on the cultural and ideological lens through which it is viewed. These new theories of science and philosophy pose a radical challenge to the way the world is viewed.

In the past twenty years or so an increasing number of social scientists and management theorists have adopted this new systemic view of the world. In the same way that scientific developments have focused on the wholeness of the universe, on the relational aspects that exist within it and on the manner in which matter changes in chaotic patterns, organisational theorists have focused their attentions on the transformational aspects of organisations, on how disorder leads to order and on how positive and negative feedback loops operate within organisations. But for many people involved in organisational development this new paradigm represents uncharted waters. This resistance to a new focus is put succinctly by Margaret Wheatley:

> We social scientists are trying hard to be conscientious, using the methodologies and thought patterns of seventeenth-century science, while the scientists, travelling away from us at the speed of light, are moving into a universe that suggests entirely new ways of understanding. Just when social scientists seem to have gotten the science down and can construct strings of variables in impressive formulae, the scientists have left, plunging ahead into the vast "porridge of being" that describes a new reality (Wheatley, 1992, p. 141).

Although this corpus of organisational theory has only been developed over the past 20–25 years it has had a profound influence on the way we manage and lead organisations. It is now an established fact that the great majority of nature's systems are driven by chaotic feedback mechanisms and that they positively use turbulent behaviour to change and develop in a creative manner. Given the complex environments in which many organisations (e.g. schools) operate, it is reasonable to think that certain aspects of chaos theory, or what is more precisely described as soft-systems theory, provides a more useful explanation of the dynamics of management than any of the more conventional models.

Implications for Leadership

As suggested earlier, in any organisation there is a strong feedback loop between management paradigm and leadership style; leadership style will influence and inform the choice of management paradigm and, in turn, through a process of feedback, this will influence and inform the style of leadership. While leadership has proven itself to be a difficult entity to define, variously described as charisma, a set of principles, a managerial process, a matter of character, something learned through study of historical leaders, etc., it is generally accepted that good management involves leadership in some format. Whereas in the past, studies in leadership have focused on the personality and power-brokering traits of leaders in the context of goal achievement, recent studies in organisational theory have focused on two paradigms of leadership: transactional and transformational.

It was suggested earlier that hard-systems, rationalist organisational paradigms develop hierarchical systems of leadership and control as a response to the diversity which may manifest itself in the organisation from time to time. This is clearly the preferred method in military establishments. The US Naval Academy defines leadership as:

> The art, science, or gift by which a person is enabled and privileged to direct the thoughts, plans and actions of others in such a manner as to obtain and command their obedience, their confidence, their respect and their loyal co-operation (Montor, 1984, p. 1).

The same manual makes it clear that the navy is a closed system, which wishes to control in the strictest sense possible any outside influences which may encroach on it; the general purpose is that the officer corps will control all transactions between it and "the hands".

Robert Starratt offers the following observations on the essential differences between transactional and transformational leadership:

> Transactional leadership usually involves an exchange of some kind, a granted request here for a future request there, a vote on this in return for a vote on that. . . . The transactional leader ensures that procedures by which people enter into these transactions are clear, aboveboard, and take into account the rights and needs of the people involved. . . . Transformational leadership, on the other hand, seeks to unite people in the pursuit of communal interests beyond their individual interests. . . . Transformational leadership calls members' attention to the basic purpose of the organisation, to the relationship between the organisation and the society it serves. Transforming leadership attempts to elevate members' self-centered attitudes, values and beliefs to higher, altruistic attitudes, values and beliefs (Starratt, 1993, p. 7).

Transactional leadership can be associated with the conventional management paradigm set out above. It relies on the skillful use of power, rewards, and contingencies to maintain or marginally improve performance and to ensure compliance with organisational policies. It results in what some theorists describe as "first-order change", i.e. a minimalist response to predictable variations in the environment.

The polar contrast to this is transformational leadership which can be associated with the systemic approach to organisational management described above. Transformational leadership engages in "second-order change" or innovation, sets out core values, describes new, exciting, sometimes unattainable goals. Following the chaotic paradigm of management, it sets out, within the boundaries of the paradigm, to engage in a programme of destruction from which new forms will emerge.

In the context of Irish education today, the implications of this body of theory are not at all clear; at first glance it would seem that hard-systems/transactional leadership and soft-systems/transformational leadership are dichotomous. The general impression one gets in reviewing the literature available is that one theory seeks to oust the other. A minority view put forward by Cavaleri and Obloj suggests that there is room for both in what they describe as "synergetic managerial tool" (Cavaleri, 1993, p. 305). In this construct, transactional and transformational leadership exist in a complementary relationship where "waves of transactional leadership must be punctuated with islands of transformations" (Ibid., p. 307).

It seems that the ideas of transformational leadership, particularly as set out by Starratt and Sergiovanni, are gaining in currency in the area of educational administration, yet many areas of contradiction and even conflict still prevail. The White Paper on Irish Education, while setting out many principles which are in tune with a systemic approach to organisational management, contained many proposals which will be seen as hierarchical and closed in character. Sergiovanni (1996, p. 41) suggests that we have much to learn from Chaos Theory which will be applicable in a school setting, although he stops short of saying that it provides a full working theory for the schoolhouse. Much of what Sergiovanni has to say in developing his *gemeinschaft* (community) theory of school leadership is borrowing on the systemic notion of inter relationships which is central to Chaos Theory.

Conclusion

This paper has attempted to describe the main ideas contained in conventional and systemic approaches to organisational management, showing the connection between those paradigms and various scientific and philosophical movements. It has suggested that both paradigms will influence greatly the type of leadership practised in an organisation. In the context of Irish education, the debate is ongoing as to which paradigm will acquire primacy. This writer would suggest that we are at a watershed at the moment, awaiting as we do the implementation of the Education Act (1998) while at the same time experiencing a growing influence of local community-based partnerships in our schools. On the one hand, there are those who will want to see education as a stabilising, predictable, traditional and safe institution in our society. On the other, there will be those wanting change, innovation and transformation. New theories in science have taught us that we cannot introduce change to a system without influencing the totality of relations within the system.

Finally, the writer is struck by the vivid image evoked by Margaret Wheatley's expression, "the porridge of being". In this regard the reader should note that the best porridge is made from very hard pin-head oats, grown organically without the aid of artificial fertilisers. For best results they require very slow cooking, or preferably, overnight soaking before being introduced to heat — those involved in educational management should know this recipe!

Endnote

[1] Braverman (1974) gives a detailed account of the development of the division of labour in the industrial workplace throughout the nineteenth century industrial revolution and on into the twentieth century. He examines very closely the work done by Frederick W. Taylor in developing his theories of scientific management. His conclusion is that the division of labour has led to the degradation of work and consequently the degradation of the worker. In Braverman's view this degradation arises from the subdivision of the work into a series of meaningless tasks, the control of the worker, the institutionalisation of the workplace, the absolute determination by the manager of the amount of time to be spent performing each task, the enforcement of rules which are very often unexplained and meaningless to the worker, the setting of production minimums, payment on the basis of output and the dictation to the worker of the precise manner in which the work is to be performed. Braverman sees the inculcation of a spirit of enterprise through appealing to the worker's sense of greed as being central to this process. From the management point of view this process is generally regarded as benign and one which allows the worker to achieve to the best of his/her ability. In Braverman's view this system of degradation takes no account of the needs of the worker or the society. It could be argued that there is a noticeable, if somewhat alarming, similarity between the system espoused by the school of scientific management and the target-achieving, exam-oriented aspects of our education system.

References

Adorno, T.W. and Horkheimer, M. (1973), *Dialectic of Enlightenment*, London: Allen Lane.

Braverman, H. (1974), *Labor and Monopoly Capital*, New York: Monthly Review Press.

Capra, Fritjof (1983), *The Turning Point: Science, Society and the Rising Culture*, New York: Bantam.

Cavaleri, Steven and Obloj, K. (1993), *Management Systems: A Global Perspective*, Belmont, CA: Wadsworth.

Hume, David (1748), *An Inquiry Concerning Human Understanding*, New York: Bobbs-Merrill (1955).

Jones, R.V. (1973), "Command and Complementarity", London: The Fourth J.D. Bernal Lecture delivered at Birbeck College.

Kvist, P. (1982), *Leadership in Schools*, Sheffield City Polytechnic.

Laszlo, Ervin (1972), *The Systems View of the World*, Oxford: Blackwell.

Montor, K. (ed.) (1984), *Fundamentals of Naval Leadership*, Annapolis, MD: Naval Institute Press.

Scileppi, John (1984), *A Systems View of Education*, London: University Press of America.

Sergiovanni, Thomas (1992), *Moral Leadership*, San Francisco: Jossey-Bass Publishers.

Sergiovanni, Thomas (1996), *Leadership for the Schoolhouse*, San Francisco: Jossey-Bass Publishers.

Smyth, J. (ed.) (1986), *Critical Perspectives on Educational Leadership*, London: Falmer Press.

Stacey, Ralph D. (1991), *The Chaos Frontier*, Oxford: Butterworth Heinemann.

Stacey, Ralph D. (1993), *Strategic Management and Organisational Dynamics*, London: Pitman.

Starratt, Robert (1993), *The Drama of Leadership*, London: Falmer Press.

Starratt, Robert (1994), "The Drama of Educational Leadership", A public lecture in October 1994, in commemoration of the late Ms. Valerie English, Dublin.

Wheatley, Margaret (1992), *Leadership and the New Science*, San Francisco: Berrett-Koehler Publishers.

Wittgenstein, L. (1953), *Philosophical Investigations*, Trans. G.E.M. Anscombe. Oxford: Blackwell.

11

Computers in the Classroom: A Question of Control

Brian Trench

A promotional video produced by Microsoft presents visions of the use of computers and of online networks in 2003–4. One sequence shows a mother and son at home in the morning. From an on-screen menu matching her recorded preferences, mother selects a television programme to watch while her son, Jackson, does last-minute work on an assignment for school. Following links from the Internet site of his local university to one of a museum in Mexico, he collates material on pre-Colombian art. Still working on the assignment due for presentation in school that morning, he searches for sellers of art replicas.

As Microsoft founder Bill Gates explained at the Dublin launch of Windows 95:

> the system did a search for him based on his criteria and actually came up and gave him the name of the place and showed him a map and told him what kind of products are available. Now we have got Jackson interested in making that purchase.

Moving seamlessly from education to commercial consumption and back again, Gates went on to declare that education was the sector in which the new computer and communications technologies can have the greatest impact. But in his vision there is a close relationship between the application of these technologies to educational innovation and their application to constructing what Gates calls "the perfect marketplace".

In considering the role of computers in the classroom, it is difficult to avoid the presence of Bill Gates. He was at the side of Gerhard Schröder in February 1999 when the German Chancellor announced his government's plans to bring all schools online by 2001 and to spend £50 million on improving computer literacy in German schools.

That same month, Gates told 4,500 delegates at the annual conference of the American Association of School Administrators that the personal computer and the Internet were:

> catalysts for reaching the educational goals that parents, educators and government have set for K–12 schools. . . . School leaders who embrace technology as a new teaching and learning tool will shape education in the twenty-first century.

In October 1997, Bill Gates was with Tony Blair when the British prime minister announced the ambitious National Grid for Learning to which all 32,000 schools in Britain are to be linked by 2002. The British government committed £50 million a year to help schools buy computers provided they raise matching funding or sponsorship. Education minister Kim Howells has stated that "if kids are not computer-literate, it's almost as bad as them being illiterate or innumerate".

Many countries around the world have initiated major programmes of accelerated investment in information and communication technologies (ICTs) for schools. In Italy, the government is supplying 150,000 computers to schools and training 100,000 teachers. The Mexican government's ScholarNet programme envisages the establishment of 20,000-35,000 computer laboratories in schools over five years; each lab contains between seven and 27 computers. In Japan, the government and the telecommunications company NTT are working together on a project to supply 900,000 computers to schools and connect all schools to the Internet. As part of its plan to become the world's "most wired" country, Canada has allocated about £100 million to expanding its SchoolNet and Community Access programmes: 16,000 schools and 34,000 public libraries were to be online by the end of March 1999.

Government leaders of social democratic orientation have been the most enthusiastic in pushing accelerated technology programmes in schools. In many cases, they have also thereby facilitated closer involvement of the corporate sector in schools. There may be a happy coincidence of interests. There may be an equitable balance of an educational interest in ensuring that teachers and students have the widest range of relevant resources to support learning, a national economic interest in ensuring that the future workforce is comfortable and competent with computer-based technologies and a commercial interest in promoting the development of the education sector as a market for equipment and services. But such a balance is, at best, unusual; the neat fit between companies' civic activities and their business goals must raise questions as to who benefits most.

Not all of those with business interests in computers and in the Internet are as unconditionally enthusiastic as Microsoft about the gains to be made for education. Alan Sugar, who brought us the Amstrad, and now owns Viglen, a computer manufacturer which targets the education market, is concerned about the "hype about the Net's use in education". Sugar fears that the focus may be taken away from "grassroots methods in education". In a scenario he proposed of two students in a school library, one with a PC connected to the Net and the other without, both being asked to obtain information for their chemistry examination on copper, "the bookworm wins hands down".

It is striking, by contrast, that in the Microsoft video mentioned above, Jackson at no time looks at, or appears to consider looking at, a book. He is depicted producing a project — which he later presents on-screen, and to strong approval from his teacher — without giving any time to understanding its substance.

In her most recent book, *Release 2.1*, described as "a design for living in the digital age", Internet entrepreneur Esther Dyson emphasises the role of the teacher in encouraging students to find out things, but also to think critically and ethically about what they find out, particularly on the Internet. The teacher, she says, motivates the student:

> to question and understand the motivations of the people and companies who post information and advertising, to observe others' intellectual property and privacy rights, and to safeguard your own.

Dyson observes that the Net is "good at showing that things are related, but not how". You can get into trouble very easily on the Net, she adds: "there still needs to be someone to guide you".

Increasingly, in schools technology initiatives, the emphasis has been placed on the role of teachers as mentors, guides and critics. The CyberSmart! School Program started in 1998 aims to promote safe use of the Internet, educating children about privacy, respecting copyrighted materials, and the ethics of communicating in the online world.

Coming later than many others to schools technology programmes, Ireland has the opportunity and the obligation to learn from the experience of earlier movers. Dyson believes the US experience indicates strongly that spending on these programmes should be considered as consisting of three roughly equal parts: hardware, software and services, and teacher training. There is a strong tendency to under-estimate the significance of the last part, Dyson says. The School Inspectors' report in Britain and the annual report of the CEO Forum in the United States both indicated in March 1999 that the training of teachers in using computer technology had been inadequate. Here, too, IT businesses have been active. Microsoft claims that its teacher training initiatives have reached more than one million teachers worldwide.

The Irish government's Schools IT2000 programme represents a commitment of £40 million from the exchequer to be spent over three years, the single most concentrated investment in schools resources in recent decades. Of this amount, 60 per cent, or £24 million, will go on equipment, software and wiring, with the balance being spent on training, curriculum resources and support. Over the life of the programme, 60,000 computers are to be supplied to schools by the end of 2001, and 20,000 teachers are to receive training in the educational use of information and communication technologies (ICTs).

Under the heading "Why Action Is Needed", the Schools IT2000 policy statement points first to Ireland's reported low ranking "in terms of its state of preparedness for the information age". This is not the place for a discussion on the terms, "information age" or "information society". But in a statement of educational policy it should be acknowledged that such discussion is possible. The unquestioning assumption that there is a widely shared view on "preparedness for the information age" is not a sound basis for any social policy. The statement that "those nations that successfully embrace the information age will gain an advantage over their competitors" is not as self-evidently meaningful as it is made to appear.

The Schools IT2000 policy document outlines four types of benefits from greater use of ICTs in schools:

1. **Social benefits**: reducing the risk of a new division between "information haves and have-nots" by ensuring equal access to new technologies for all young people;

2. **Vocational and economic benefits**: making young people familiar with ICTs will make them more employable and help sustain Ireland's growth;

3. **Pedagogic benefits**: using ICTs to enhance the educational experience "by providing rich, exciting and motivating environments" and promoting "creativity, imagination and self-expression";

4. **Catalytic benefits**: using ICTs to promote emphasis on information handling over memorising facts.

Each of these points has much to recommend it, though none is self-sufficient. The claimed social and educational advantages can be realised only if there are accompanying changes in the pattern of educational resource provision, in the culture of the educational system and in syllabi and curricula. For example, we can expect that existing social divisions within education will be hardened rather than lessened through the provision of ICTs in schools unless there are formal and explicit measures to correct current and emerging distortions. On the claimed teaching benefits of using ICTs, it seems almost trite, but necessary, to remark that it is teachers, the curriculum and the school ethos, much more than the equipment, who determine whether students are motivated and stimulated to express themselves imaginatively.

Schools IT2000 refers to international experience as supporting its case on the advantages to be derived from applying ICTs more intensively within schools. But the lessons of that experience appear to be more complex than is suggested: a study of Californian school students showed no strong link between academic performance and the level of computer provi-

sion in schools, though it did suggest that benefits were greater
in schools in lower-income areas. The American magazine *Atlantic Monthly* has commented that:

> there is no good evidence that most uses of computers
> significantly improve teaching and learning, yet school
> districts are cutting programmes — music, art, physical
> education — to make way for this dubious nostrum.

In Ireland, as elsewhere, the push for accelerated supply of
computers to schools came from outside the education sector.
The then Taoiseach John Bruton visited a relatively well
equipped school in his Meath constituency in late 1996 just as
the draft report of the Information Society Steering Committee
reached the government. Excited by the sight of students gathering and sharing information via the Internet, Bruton directed his ministers each to come up with proposals for putting
an information society policy into effect. The one major part
that took shape before the government lost power was what
became Schools IT2000.

The Fianna Fáil-led government enthusiastically took over
the programme from its predecessor, even "launching" it again
in November 1997 as part of its own £250 million educational
investment programme, the second time at the Taoiseach's old
school in Whitehall, Dublin. Mr Ahern was to return there a
year later with British Prime Minister Tony Blair to present a
scheme for cross-border co-operation which involves the distribution of 200 computers to 50 schools, 25 in the North and 25
in the Republic, who will work on joint projects.

The corporate sector has become heavily involved in schools
technology projects. Telecom Eireann has made its own £10
million contribution to Schools IT2000. Siemens, Microsoft, Intel, Dell, IBM, Hewlett-Packard and others have donated computers, peripherals and software to local projects and Tesco has
run a computer vouchers scheme at its stores. Launching an

educational technology project, "Reinventing Education", with Lou Gerstner, IBM's chief executive officer, the Minister for Education and Science, Micheál Martin, encouraged private companies to become "active corporate citizens in supporting education projects".

Discussion of the principles and methods of this push for more computers in schools has been muted at best. Fine Gael's education spokesperson Richard Bruton criticised Schools IT2000 as insufficient: it would provide one computer for every 14 pupils, he said; the best countries were achieving a ratio of 1:10.

There are, indeed, significant issues associated with the level of provision, but not critically related to the average allocation per school. The case can be made that spreading the provision of computers too thinly may mean that the equipment becomes more of a burden than a boon. Speaking in Dublin in the presence of the Taoiseach, Nicholas Negroponte of the Massachusetts Institute of Technology endorsed the Irish government's strong orientation to primary schools in its Schools IT2000 programme. But he went on to state that it was no solution to provide a single computer per school. Better, he said, to put 20 computers into every twentieth school, in order to achieve critical mass and promote shared learning.

The more fundamental arguments turn around the place and prominence of such initiatives within the totality of educational policy and provision. So strong is the consensus that educational technology projects are "a good thing" that it seems almost impertinent to ask how and whether the £40 million of government money going to Schools IT2000 can be justified in relation to all of the other pressing needs of primary and second-level schools. There are other programmes to improve the physical infrastructure of schools and to boost teacher numbers under way but none matches the scale and scope of Schools IT2000.

The teachers' organisations have joined in actively, developing their own projects to support the wider government-led initiative. Schools with a track record in using — and taming — computers in the classroom are responding vigorously. Some have been selected as pilots in demonstrating effective use of ICTs. Other schools in areas of social disadvantage like Dublin's inner city are receiving particular attention. But many individual teachers are nervous. The anonymous contributor to Staff Room, a column in *The Irish Times Education & Living* supplement, wrote about the arrival of a new multimedia, Internet-ready computer:

> I have the strange feeling that I'm being suckered a bit here. Greeks and gifts keep popping to mind. I know this is quite an expensive piece of machinery which has landed on my doorstep but, in truth, I never asked for it.

It is easy to imagine the excitement that John Bruton may have felt when he saw school children making connections from their classroom in Meath to far-flung places or accessing information on a wide range of topics. Many of us have seen this in our own children and students. Easy access to diverse types of information on a seemingly infinite variety of issues has an obvious attraction. The visually attractive, multi-layered presentation of information on the Web and CD-ROMs may encourage some children to engage in research who might otherwise be reluctant to do so. Adaptive technologies can make certain facets of education available for the first time or more easily to those with particular learning needs or disabilities. The structured interactivity of many "edutainment" products stimulates children to respond rapidly but coherently to sets of questions and choices and can help younger children develop their co-ordination and their ability to recognise patterns.

In order to build on these and many other possible benefits of using ICTs in the classroom we need also to be aware of the attendant risks. The benefits and risks identified in the wider international discussion around computers-for-schools programmes tend to mirror each other. Some have to do with the students' learning experiences, and others with the impact on the wider schools system.

Among the stated benefits of intensive use of computers in schools are that it will:

- Widen children's cultural horizons

- Promote shared learning through information exchange

- Encourage more active learning

- Help build students' confidence and creativity

- Ease access to education for children with disabilities

- Help reduce or overcome social disadvantage and isolation

- Reinforce through visual communication the impact of verbal and text-based instruction

- Encourage greater comfort with contemporary technology

- Prepare students better for employment

- Prepare students to be active citizens.

On the other hand, almost precisely opposed claims can be, and are, made on the risks of intensive use of computers in schools, e.g. that it will:

- Reduce students' interest in reading

- Discourage reflection and assimilation of information

- Inhibit the development of creativity

- Encourage a more passive attitude to learning

- Expose children to the risk of Net addiction

- Increase social isolation

- Expose children to harmful material

- Promote a false association between computer competence and educational ability

- Add a new layer of social advantage and disadvantage

- Give new force to competition between schools

- Pressure parents to buy computers for homes.

Evidence that Internet access in schools can raise children's awareness of a wider world around them can be seen on the Web site of Coolderry Central National School in County Offaly. Pupils of that school, as of many others, kept in touch with explorer Tim Severin as he sailed around the Spice Islands during 1997 and posted some of the messages sent and received on the school's Web site.

In March 1999, more than two million students across the United States linked up with explorer Robert Ballard in the Amazon Basin in Peru. Ballard broadcast live from the jungle via the Jason project, bringing some of the sights and sounds of the South American rainforest to North American classrooms. The claim made for the Jason project is that it has:

> pioneered real-time interactive distance learning, pushing the technology envelope to find new ways to engage students in scientific exploration.

Primary schools in Dublin and second-level schools in Donegal have built relationships with counterparts in France and Canada. Some of these relationships lead to physical visits, like that of a schoolgirl from Alaska to Dromore National School, in Killygordon, County Donegal. A school in Baldoyle, County Dublin, Pobal Scoil Neasain, has been linked to schools in six EU states through a partly Web-based project on children's ideas of science.

Web access opens up connections to many well-conceived and -executed online resources, notably in science and technology. From several decades of Internet use in science and technology have grown myriad public education and schools-oriented projects which are mediated through the Web. This culture of information exchange is visibly affecting schools too, some of which have provided resources for use by others. On the Web site of St Enda's College in Galway, for example, there is a valuable and well-presented guide to astronomy. The site of a Canadian school provides a gateway to a wide range of resources on physical and natural sciences.

Nicholas Negroponte has insisted that learning on the Internet contributes importantly to children's socialisation. "All the evidence in the world points to the fact that children increase their social and communication skills by spending time on the Net," he said in an interview with a European Commission publication, *RTD Info*. Professor Niki Davis of Exeter University in England has also said that computers used in groups can enhance social skills.

Negroponte goes further in stating that computer communications can be a means of overcoming social disadvantage. Through a non-profit body, 2B1, the MIT professor and like-minded colleagues promote the provision of computers to schools in the world's poorest countries, focusing on access to global communications, via satellite, from rural areas.

In more advanced countries, governments and businesses have supported initiatives aimed at ensuring that those in disadvantaged groups and areas have access to computer technologies. Under the Dublin Inner City Schools Computerisation project, 20 city schools will receive computers donated by Siemens and technical and training support. In the poorer areas of Washington DC, software developer Oracle Corporation has helped provide computers to minority and economically disadvantaged schools. Volunteers from the company, along with volunteers from non-government organisations, have been installing the equipment, training the teachers and providing technical support. This initiative is part of Oracle Promise, a $100 million project to help bridge the "digital divide".

On the other hand, the drive to equip schools with computers may produce new expressions of social and regional divides. As long ago as 1992, the Apple specialist magazine *MacWorld* reported on the basis of a series of visits to US schools that "computers simply perpetuate a two-tier system of education for rich and poor". In a published debate with David Wimpress, chairman of UK NetYear, journalist Paul Fisher argued that "the only justification for school computing is to give the poorest children some access". Most children do not need particular instruction in computers because they "learn to use computers willy-nilly, on videos, game consoles and home computers", he wrote.

Where the parents associated with a particular school can afford to do so, they may contribute to ensuring that competitive advantage — otherwise, social disadvantage — is maintained by supporting computer purchases from their own resources. Teachers report that parents are increasingly asking for reassurance that their children's school is up to speed. According to a survey by computer makers Compaq, more than two-thirds of parents in Britain were convinced of the educational benefits of home computers, but more than half of them said they knew less about computers than their children did. *The Sunday Times* described a parents' day at a "pricey" school in Britain:

> Laid out in the school's shiny new Information Technology department, sharply suited salesmen from Compaq, IBM and Toshiba are proudly displaying the latest essential equipment for every school child's satchel: portable notebook computers, with Pentium processors and colour screens, at £2,000 apiece.

As to the impact of computers on the educational experience, there is "a danger that young people may come to envisage school work as the assembling of vast quantities of information from the Internet which they fail to assimilate", according to Dr Kevin Williams, lecturer in the Mater Dei Institute, Dublin. Writing in *The Irish Times*, he argued that "the time some students spend on-line would be more fruitfully spent getting to grips with the basic concepts as these are explained in lectures".

Science fiction writer Ray Bradbury has described the Internet as being like a pinball machine. He argued against putting computers into schools before the second or third grade, saying that he would advise his grandchildren, who are growing up in a world where the Internet is ever-present: "Go to the library".

American educational psychologist Jane Healy, a former "techno-pusher" by her own admission, has come to the conclusion that children under seven gain nothing, and may lose a lot, by being exposed to computers. In a recent book, *Failure to Connect*, she states that creativity scores of pre-school children using so-called accelerative software dropped by 50 per cent in a short time. Healy says computers are not inherently better than television; both can be equally mind-numbing if used in the wrong way.

Dependence on computers and on television may reinforce one another. TV programmes targeted at children frequently broadcast a Web address at which further information about the programme can be found. What children often look for first, and most, on the Web is information about favourite television personalities and programmes.

David Squires, a lecturer in educational computing at King's College London, has identified weaknesses in some educational software which he describes as hindering the learning of creative skills and encouraging passivity. Critically, he notes that such software shows flaws which the presence of a teacher could alleviate.

Internet addiction is an increasingly widely acknowledged phenomenon, affecting adults as well as children. *Caught in the Web*, a study of Internet addiction by Dr Kimberly Young of the University of Pittsburgh, contains stories such as that of the 12-year-old boy who ran up a phone bill of £800 and shot his mother when she cancelled his Net connection.

None of these observations or arguments supports a case for doing less in this area. They may, however, point to a need to do things differently and to question the assumptions on which the current major investment projects are based. The very fact that the arguments on the benefits and risks of more intensive use of computers in schools are balanced as they are indicates, above all, that everything depends on how the technology is used rather than on the technology itself. The roles of teachers and parents are crucial — and it is not yet too late to develop the views on what each is expected to do.

If computers are to be used effectively in the classroom, hierarchical pedagogic methods are challenged. Computers are not just new tools for doing the old job, not just another, more efficient, means to pour information into students' heads. The training of teachers in relation to educational technology should be concentrated on equipping them to guide their students in making discriminating use of frequently seductive software and services. Students need guidance in identifying reliable information sources, in recognising valid arguments, in sifting and sorting the masses of frequently useless information they may now have at their disposal.

For the present, most attention is focused on the technology aspects of providing computers and ensuring they are connected. But by contrast with the need to ensure that schools provide an environment in which information is handled with care, the technical side of the training is relatively trivial. Indeed, some of the obstacles to a clearer view of how computers might be used beneficially could be removed by devolving technical responsibilities to support teams working with clusters of schools.

In the 1960s and 1970s, much of the concern about wider use of computers related to the displacement of workers through automation. In the current phase, and in education in particular, more intensive use of computers requires more, not less, human involvement. It may also require reshaping of roles and relationships in the educational system.

The challenge to teachers and to the schools system is to assert and to develop the educational rationale and the teaching and learning context for technology projects. Individual schools have been encouraged to do this, and many are demonstrating good practice. The National Centre for Technology in Education has an important role in evaluating products and in developing models for their effective use. But the bigger picture is crudely drawn and some of the orientations are questionable. If the educational priorities are not clearly established, it is possible that a great deal of money could be spent without any measurable or significant gains to the quality of education.

12

Barriers to Entering Higher Education[*]

Patrick Clancy

Why are we Concerned about Access to Higher Education?

It is appropriate to start by presenting a brief justification for our concern with the issue of access to higher education. Our interest in educational opportunity is linked to the central role which education plays in the status attainment process and in the reward structure of society. This development is, in turn, related to rapid changes in the occupational structure with a growth in employment opportunities for those with technical and professional qualifications and the demise of employment opportunities for those who lack advanced education and training. The importance of inheritance has declined as a determinant of future status with a sharp reduction in the number of young people who enter family employment with the prospect of inheritance. Increasingly, educational qualifications have become *the* currency for employment. Such has been the transformation that, increasingly, education is being viewed as a form of cultural or knowledge-based capital which is analo-

[*] An earlier version of this paper was presented at the Union of Students in Ireland's *Disadvantaged Access Conference*, in Dublin Castle, 4 March 1998.

gous to economic capital. The operational measure of this capital is the amount and quality of educational qualifications which one possesses.

Moreover, it is not simply the case that educational qualifications serve as a screening device which allocates people to their respective position in a hierarchical labour market, but the absence of valued educational credentials leads to a very high risk of unemployment. There is some evidence that this link between educational qualifications and employment is more rigid in Ireland than in other countries as illustrated in Table 1 which shows the relationship between level of education and the rate of unemployment among the adult population in OECD countries. While, in 1995, the level of unemployment in Ireland was higher than the mean for all OECD countries, the Irish rate was lower than the country mean for all third level graduates. A disproportionately high level of unemployment in Ireland is heavily concentrated among those who have not completed second-level education. In Ireland, the differential between the unemployment rate for those with university education and those with incomplete secondary is more than twice that of the average for all countries.

Table 1: Unemployment Rates by Level of Educational Attainment, Ireland and All OECD Countries

Level of Education	Ireland	All OECD Countries
Below Upper Secondary	16.4	10.1
Upper Secondary	7.6	7.0
Non-university Tertiary	5.0	5.6
University Level Education	3.4	4.0
All Levels of Education	10.7	7.3

Source: Adapted from OECD, 1997.

A second aspect of the relationship between education and employment is the rate of return on investment in education. Recent research suggests that, in Ireland, the average private rate of return to a year's additional schooling is about 8 per cent (Callan and Harman, 1997). This rate appears to be towards the upper end of the range of findings from international studies. Although still positive, there is some evidence that the rate of return for younger age groups may be declining, relative to that for older age groups. The main exception here is for degree-level qualifications where the rate of return is highest for the younger age groups.

Quite apart from the instrumental aspect of higher education being viewed as an investment which yields economic returns, it is also the case that higher education is increasingly viewed as a consumption good which is as much concerned with "life styles" as with "life chances". In a situation where middle class participation is becoming almost universal, those denied access to the college culture can feel disenfranchised and marginalised. There is a danger in our increasingly materialistic society that this cultural aspect of higher education is overlooked. It needs to be stressed that access to higher education offers great potential for personal development and cultural enrichment. Thus, higher education has the potential to impact on both the quality of the individual's life and the collective life of a community.

Selectivity in Higher Education?

The enormous expansion in participation in post-compulsory education in recent decades can be seen as a direct consequence of the changes in economic and occupational structure which we have alluded to above. In this respect the Irish experience is broadly similar to that of most other Western countries. It has been suggested that this enrolment growth will

perhaps stand as *the* trend of the post-war period which histo-
rians will chronicle and debate in future years. Currently, in
the Republic of Ireland about 84 per cent of the age cohort are
staying on to Leaving Certificate level and about 50 per cent of
the age cohort are going on to full-time higher education. Over
the past 30 years there has been an approximately five-fold increase in enrolments in higher education. Full-time enrolments
in higher education in Ireland have increased from 20,698 in
1965/66 to 102,662 by 1995/96 (Table 2). This quantitative
growth has been accompanied by a diversification of higher
education with a dramatic increase in the size of the technological sector, growing from five per cent of enrolments in the
mid-1960s to 37 per cent in the mid-1990s.

**Table 2: Enrolment of Full-time Students in Higher Edu-
cation by Sector, 1965/66 and 1995/96**

	1965/66	1995/96
	%	%
Universities*	77.3	55.4
Institutes of Technology	4.9	37.1
Colleges of Education**	6.9	0.6
Other Colleges	10.9	6.9
Total %	100.0	100.0
Total no.	20,698	102,662

*　Includes RCSI and, for 1995/96 only, NCAD.

**　Enrolments of BEd students (n=994) in the two largest Colleges of Educa-
tion are included in the university sector in 1995/96.

However, our concern here is not with overall growth but with
the question of who benefits from the expansion. The monitoring of socio-economic inequalities in access to higher education
in Ireland was first addressed in the landmark *Investment in
Education* (1966) report. In more recent times the issue has

been examined in successive national surveys which have been funded by the Higher Education Authority. The most recent study relates to those who entered third-level education in 1992 (Clancy, 1995). This study found large disparities by so-cio-economic group. Thirty-eight per cent of higher education entrants came from the four highest socio-economic groups (Higher Professional, Lower Professional, Employers and Man-agers, and Salaried Employees) although these groups consti-tuted less than 21 per cent of the relevant population. In con-trast, the five lowest socio-economic groups (Other Non-Manual, Skilled, Semi-Skilled and Unskilled Manual, and Other Agricultural Occupations) were seriously under-represented; 35 per cent of entrants came from these groups although they constituted almost 56 per cent of the relevant age cohort.

Notwithstanding the persistence of high levels of socio-economic group inequality, a comparison of the most recent findings with those from 1980 and 1986 reveals some reduction in inequality. This is illustrated in Table 3 which presents *es-timates* of the proportion of the age cohort in each socio-economic group going on to higher education in 1980, 1986 and 1992. During a time of expanding enrolments it is no surprise to find that most socio-economic groups experienced an in-crease in the proportion going on to higher education. For the four highest socio-economic groups the proportion going was in excess of a half in 1992 and for the Higher Professional group it was 89 per cent, having risen from an estimated two-thirds in 1980. All of the under-represented socio-economic groups experienced an increase in the proportion entering higher edu-cation. For the Other Non-Manual and Skilled Manual groups it had risen from 9 per cent in 1980 to 26 per cent by 1992, while for the combined groups of Unskilled and Semi-Skilled Manual it had increased from 5 per cent in 1980 to 14 per cent in 1992.

Table 3: Estimated Proportion of Age Cohort Entering Full-time Higher Education by Fathers' Socio-Economic Group in 1980, 1986 and 1992

Socio-Economic Group	1992	1986	1980
Farmers	.49	.36	.24
Other Agricultural Occupations	.22	.12	.04
Higher Professional	.89	.75	.67
Lower Professional	.53	.54	.38
Employers and Managers	.67	.43	.48
Salaried Employees	.53	.58	.59
Intermediate Non-Manual Workers	.33	.30	.22
Other Non-Manual Workers	.26	.11	.09
Skilled Manual Workers	.26	.13	.09
Semi-Skilled Manual Workers	.16	.11	.09
Unskilled Manual Workers	.13	.04	.03
Total	.36	.25	.20

Source: Clancy (1995).

There is no entirely satisfactory way of quantifying the degree of reduction (if any) in inequality which has occurred over the period of the three surveys. One method which has gained acceptance in the international literature is the use of *odds ratios*. For example, if we compare the changes between 1980 and 1992 in the participation ratios of the two groups with the highest admission rates (Higher Professional and Employer and Managers) and the two groups with the lowest admission rates (Semi-Skilled and Unskilled Manual) we find that there has been a reduction in inequality of 22 per cent over the twelve-year period. If instead of comparing the two highest and two lowest socio-economic groups we calculate a single rate of admission for the six groups which were "over-represented" in

1980 and the five groups which were "under-represented" and compare these rates of admission with those which prevailed in 1992 the odds ratio was reduced by 36 per cent. Thus, in both of these comparisons, the use of the odds ratio suggests that there has indeed been a significant reduction in inequality over the past twelve years.

In addition to documenting overall levels of selectivity in higher education the three national surveys have shown how this is complemented by further selectivity by sector and field of study. The more prestigious the sector and field of study the greater the social inequality in participation levels. Within the university sector the higher professional groups had their strongest representation, while students from working class backgrounds had their lowest representation in this sector. There was further differentiation within the university sector with the Higher Professional group being especially strongly represented within the faculties of Architecture, Medicine and Law while the Semi-Skilled and Unskilled Manual groups had their highest proportionate representation in Education and Social Science. In contrast, while there continued to be disparities between the socio-economic groups in the pattern of access to the RTCs (Institutes of Technology), the degree of inequality was significantly less than in the other sectors. All of the Manual socio-economic groups had their highest representation in this sector (Clancy, 1995).

Of course, class differences in access to higher education represent merely the end stage of a cumulative process which begins at pre-school level and is manifest through primary and post-primary education. To secure a place in third-level education we can identify three separate transitions which must be made. The first crucial transition requires students to stay in school until the end of the second-level cycle to take the Leaving Certificate. The second transition requires students to reach the level of attainment necessary to qualify for a third-level place. The third transition relates to the final decision to take a third-level place — this decision is limited to those who both survive to Leaving Certificate level and who achieve the necessary level of attainment to secure a third-level place. The present author has documented these transitions in research which was done for the Technical Working Group (1995) which supported the Steering Committee on the Future Development of Higher Education. The research was based on a combined analysis of the findings from three successive School Leavers' surveys, 1991-93. These data allow us to examine the inter-relationship between school leavers' socio-economic group, educational level and attainment, and destination upon leaving school.

Table 4 shows the education levels of school leavers by socio-economic groups. If, for example, we look at the percentage of school leavers who leave school with no qualifications we notice that in the case of the Higher Professional group this is less than 1 per cent, while 16 per cent of the children from Un-skilled Manual Workers' families leave with no qualifications. In contrast, if we look at the percentages from the different social groups which leave school with a Leaving Certificate, for the Higher Professional group it is 97 per cent, whereas for the Unskilled Manual group it is under 53 per cent. Thus, as far as access to higher education is concerned, the first transition — remaining in school long enough to sit the Leaving Certificate — is highly class-specific.

Table 4: Percentage Distribution of School Leavers by Educational Level and Fathers' Socio-economic Group

Educational Level					
Father's Socio-economic Group	No Qualification	Junior/ Inter/ Group	Leaving Cert	Total	Total
	%	%	%	%	N
Farmers	2.7	13.9	83.8	100	950
Other Agricultural	12.3	24.7	63.0	100	146
Higher Professional	0.0	2.9	97.1	100	315
Lower Professional	0.4	3.4	95.7	100	233
Employers and Managers	1.8	7.8	90.7	100	679
Salaried Employees	1.6	4.7	93.2	100	191
Intermediate Non-manual	3.5	11.9	84.3	100	402
Other Non-manual	7.7	21.7	70.5	100	770
Skilled Manual	5.9	18.1	75.9	100	1,367
Semi-skilled Manual	9.9	28.4	61.7	100	162
Unskilled Manual	16.2	31.2	52.5	100	628
Unknown	32.4	18.9	48.6	100	37
TOTAL	5.8	16.3	77.8	100	5,880

The second transition relates to the level of attainment in the Leaving Certificate. As we have already noted it is not sufficient merely to stay in school long enough to sit the examination, one must also attain a good level of achievement in the Leaving Certificate if one hopes to qualify for a place in higher education. Again, at this transition there are clear class differences in attainment level for those who sit the Leaving Certificate. These differences are reported in Table 5. Here, if we examine those with less than 5 passes in the Leaving Certificate we notice that the percentages for the Unskilled and Semi-Skilled Manual groups are 11 per cent and 12 per cent, respectively, while less than 1 per cent of the Professional groups fall within this category. The class differences are even more dramatic if we look at percentages who achieve 5 or more honours (i.e. those with grade C or higher on a higher level paper). For the Higher Professional groups it is 55 per cent, while for the Unskilled Manual it is less than 8 per cent.

Table 5: Percentage Distribution of School Leavers Who Sat the Leaving Certificate by Level of Attainment and Fathers' Socio-economic Group

Socio-economic Group	<5 Passes	5+ Passes	1 Honour	2-4 Honours	5+ Honours	Total	
	%	%	%	%	%	%	N
Farmers	4.1	20.1	16.2	39.6	20.1	**100**	753
Other Agricultural	5.7	38.6	13.6	21.6	17.0	**100**	88
Higher Professional	0.7	6.3	7.3	30.8	54.5	**100**	286
Lower Professional	0.9	9.8	11.6	35.8	41.9	**100**	215
Employers and Managers	3.6	15.1	11.8	39.7	30.0	**100**	577
Salaried Employees	2.9	20.5	12.3	35.7	28.7	**100**	171

Intermedi-ate Non-manual	4.3	19.7	12.6	42.2	21.2	**100**	325
Other Non-manual	5.7	36.0	12.9	33.1	12.3	**100**	505
Skilled Manual	6.5	33.8	16.3	31.0	12.4	**100**	990
Semi-skilled Manual	12.1	42.9	15.4	20.9	9.9	**100**	91
Unskilled Manual	10.9	45.1	11.6	24.6	7.8	**100**	293
Unknown	20.0	40.0	6.7	13.3	20.0	**100**	15
TOTAL	**5.1***	**25.6**	**13.6**	**34.3**	**21.5**	**100**	**4,310**

* The percentage with less that five passes differs significantly from the national figure of about 14 per cent of those who sat the Leaving Certificate Examination. Part of the difference is due to missing information on educational attainment, which seems to be disproportionately concentrated among the low achievers. In addition, since these data on achievement are self-reported there may be some grade inflation.

The third transition, which is shown in Table 6, refers to those who have sat the Leaving Certificate and achieved a minimum of 5 passes in this examination. Taking into account both the socio-economic group of origin and the level of attainment in the Leaving Certificate, this table reports the percentages going on to higher education. Overall, 44 per cent of Leaving Certificate students from the three samples transferred into higher education and it is clear that this transition is strongly influenced by both level of attainment and socio-economic group. Not surprisingly, as educational attainment increases, so too does the likelihood of proceeding to higher education. On average, only 8 per cent of those with five or more passes transferred to third level; this compares with 88 per cent of those with five or more honours.

Table 6: Percentage of School Leavers with Leaving Certificate Level of Education Who Enrolled in Higher Education by Level of Attainment in Leaving Certificate and Fathers' Socio-economic Group

Father's Socio-economic Group	5+ Passes	1 Honour	2-4 Honours	5+ Honours	Total
	%	%	%	%	%
Farmers	8.6	32.8	55.7	88.1	46.5
Other Agricultural	5.9	16.7	68.4	86.7	31.8
Higher Professional	5.6	57.1	67.0	94.2	76.6
Lower Professional	9.5	16.0	64.9	81.1	60.4
Employers and Managers	16.1	39.7	65.5	89.6	60.5
Salaried Employees	17.1	28.6	60.7	83.7	51.5
Intermediate Non-manual	6.3	26.8	62.8	85.5	48.9
Other Non-manual	7.7	16.9	46.1	88.7	30.9
Skilled Manual	8.1	21.1	55.7	82.1	35.1
Semi-skilled Manual	5.1	35.7	36.8	100	26.1
Unskilled Manual	4.5	11.8	44.4	91.3	20.5
Unknown	0.0	0.0	50.0	100	30.8
TOTAL	**8.2**	**26.5**	**57.5**	**87.8**	**44.1**

However, the pattern of transition is also influenced by fathers' socio-economic group. Of those with five or more passes (and no honours) in the Leaving Certificate the percentages going on to higher education are highest for the Employers and Managers (16 per cent), and Salaried Employees (17 per cent) groups. This represents twice the average percentage going on to higher education for all students with this level of attainment. At medium levels of attainment there are also marked differences between socio-economic groups, where, in general, the overall pattern favours those from higher socio-economic groups. However, perhaps the most interesting feature of Table 6 is the relatively little variation by socio-economic group in the enrolment rate for those with the highest level of attainment (5 or more honours). For the high achievers the effect of fathers' socio-economic group is very small, with all socio-economic groups approaching parity. Class differences, therefore, are not consistent across all levels of attainment.

Some Policy Options

In this section of the paper we will consider some policy questions which arise in the light of the research findings presented. For the most part we will confine remarks to policies which are designed to facilitate higher percentages of school leavers from disadvantaged backgrounds continuing on to higher education. There is a range of separate policies which arises in relation to providing second chance opportunities aimed at older age groups who were previously denied the possibility of entering third level. This would require a separate paper. However, in passing it should be noted that the provision for mature students entering higher education in the Republic of Ireland is extremely limited. In 1994 less than four per cent of full-time students were "mature students" and of those only a minority come from lower socio-economic groups.

In relation to school leavers we can identify three categories of student which require attention. The first category involves those who leave school early before completing second level. As we saw from our analysis of the School Leavers Survey, about 22 per cent of the age cohort fall within this category. This group of early leavers is clearly the most vulnerable and faces very poor labour market prospects. A substantial reduction in this early leaving must be a number one priority for educational policy. While some progress has been achieved in this area in recent years it remains a major problem. The NESF report on *Early School Leavers and Youth Unemployment* (1997) shows that in 1995 about 1,000 students did not transfer to post-primary, while more than 2,000 left before taking the Junior Certificate. A further 2,000 got less than five passes in the Junior Certificate, leaving a total of more than 5,000 unqualified school leavers. A further 8,000 left before taking the Leaving Certificate. Thus, more than 13,000 students were disqualified from even contemplating higher education.

The second category involves those who remain in school to take the Leaving Certificate but fail to reach the required level of attainment to secure a third-level place. And while low levels of attainment are not confined to students from lower socio-economic groups, one of the findings from the analysis of the School Leavers Survey is that the problem is disproportionately concentrated in these groups. The under-achievement of many students is directly related to their class position. Many students from disadvantaged backgrounds are simply unable to compete on equal terms in an examination system where others may have vastly superior resources. These resources include: higher family income, better educated parents, supportive peers, good study facilities, availability of grinds and repeat Leaving Certificate opportunity. Frequently the poverty of resources interacts with motivational and cultural orientations. If students from disadvantaged backgrounds believe that higher education is not a realistic option for someone in their position they are unlikely to have the same incentive to seek to maximise their academic attainment. Although there is considerable evidence on the relationship between poverty of resources and educational aspirations the two dimensions are not, of course, coterminous. For example, the very high admission rates to higher education from western counties suggest that in some communities, at least, families with quite meagre resources foster and realise high aspirations.

The third category involves those who may have met the attainment requirement but for whom the level of grant is insufficient or for whom the opportunity cost of further years in education is too great. While the numbers in this category are significantly less than in the other two, there is a need to devise a separate policy response for this group.

In respect of the first two categories of disadvantaged students mentioned above, the dominant perspective shared by educationalists and policy makers is that best results can be achieved from early intervention. This priority is reflected in a range of government initiatives of which the Early Start Programme, the Breaking the Cycle of Educational Disadvantage initiative and the Home/School/Community Liaison Scheme are the best examples. However, while acknowledging the existence of favourable attitudes towards tackling disadvantage, it is not at all certain that there is a realistic assessment of the scale of intervention which will be required if we are to make significant progress. Furthermore, it must be accepted that intervention through the educational system will not be sufficient to counteract the deep-rooted structural inequalities in society at large, inequalities which were exacerbated in the 1980s by very high levels of unemployment and increasing income differentials. Thus, the burden of tackling disadvantage must not be left to education alone.

The impact of successful intervention at pre-school and first level will be to reduce the incidence of educational failure. Such success will be reflected at second level in higher retention rates and in higher levels of academic attainment. A continuing difficulty in relation to early school leavers relates to the economic circumstances of families. If we are to make substantial progress it is felt that it will be necessary take measures which deal with the financial deprivation of families. We have to take into account not just the financial outlay which staying in education demands, but also the opportunity cost of staying in school. In other words, staying in school involves expenditure by families but it also involves foregoing the possibility of earning, however small the income may be from employment. In this context it may be appropriate to re-examine the case for special allowances for teenagers who are still in education. A possible mechanism is to make a significantly increased child benefit payment contingent on teenagers remaining at school. This is an area of policy which needs to be re-examined in the context of overall social welfare provision and the undoubted significant costs involved need to be set against the price to be paid subsequently for not intervening early to break the cycle of disadvantage. There is much to commend the proposals made by Tim Callan and his colleagues at the ESRI (Callan et al., 1994) in calling for a substantial increase in Child Benefit to a level of between £75 to £80 per month (part of the cost of which would be recouped from high and middle income taxpayers). This would seem to have real potential for facilitating educational participation from disadvantaged families. The explicit linking of significant payments to families, contingent on remaining in education, could be an important factor in facilitating higher retention rates in the post-compulsory years.

It is acknowledged that responsibility for combating disadvantage at first and second level rests primarily with those who operate these systems. However, given the fact that universities and other third-level colleges have long asserted their legitimate interests in matters such as second-level curriculum and examinations it is appropriate that they would accept some responsibility to assist in helping to combat disadvantage. Imaginative pilot programmes, such as the Ballymun Initiative on Third-level Education (BITE) — in which Dublin City University is involved — and the Limerick Community-based Education Initiative (LCBEI) — with University of Limerick involvement, have demonstrated the potential for successful interventions. These programmes such as combine a range of financial, social and cultural supports to selected pupils in the participating schools. They are, however, only pilot programmes; thus the scale of intervention is very limited and in most cases the participating schools are chosen on the basis of geographical proximity to certain third-level colleges. Some of them are also based on the principle of relatively early selection and "sponsorship" of selected students. It is difficult to envisage a national programme based on this model.

It is important that we learn from these pilot programmes and that we develop a country-wide strategy whereby all post-primary schools which cater for disadvantaged pupils will have a programme which incorporates the more successful features of these schemes. It is also desirable that such college/school linkage schemes be integrated with other initiatives which are in place to combat disadvantage. The expanding Home/School/Community Liaison Scheme and associated adult and community education schemes may offer the best prospect of mainstreaming, on a national basis, some of the cultural interventions which have been piloted by the various third-level college/school linkage programmes.

While it is accepted, on the basis of evidence from the School Leavers Surveys and from the result of international research, that the most effective interventions aimed at reducing educational failure and inequality will be made at earlier stages of the educational system, it is also necessary to look separately at the point of transition from Leaving Certificate to third level. At this stage the opportunity cost of staying in education becomes highly significant. In this context the maximum level of grant is totally inadequate for students from disadvantaged backgrounds who can expect no assistance from their parents — in reality, parents come to expect a financial contribution from their children at this stage. The maximum grant in terms of maintenance for students living away from home is £1,600, while the lowest estimates suggest that it would cost students at least twice that level to maintain themselves during the academic year. Students from disadvantaged backgrounds, who desire to stay in full-time education, need a level of grant support which enables them to maintain themselves independently of their parents. They should not find themselves significantly worse off than their peers, many of whom are in receipt of unemployment benefits. While there may be a strong case for raising the overall level of grant for all students in receipt of maintenance, it is accepted that any significant increase would have serious implications for the exchequer. However, there is an overwhelming case for the introduction of a special enhanced level of grant for students from disadvantaged families. Detailed consideration would need to be given to the determination of an appropriate income threshold below which students would qualify for an enhanced level of grant. At a minimum, it is suggested that families dependent on social welfare benefits and others with incomes at or below this level would automatically qualify for an enhanced maintenance grant. It is considered that action in this area should be the number one priority in any revamping of the student support system.

It is probable that the inadequacy of the grant system is itself a contributory factor to the lower levels of attainment at second level of those from disadvantaged backgrounds. While rising levels of attainment in the Leaving Certificate have, in recent years, been fueled by the competition for third-level places, only those for whom higher education is perceived as a realistic option have contributed to this grade inflation. For those students for whom third-level education is not perceived as being realistic there is little incentive to work for high grades.

While there is little point in revisiting this issue at this stage, it is felt that the elimination of undergraduate fees was not the most efficient use of scarce public resources for the enhancement of higher education. There was a clear need, as evidenced by my own research, to raise the income threshold governing eligibility for grants. However, on grounds of equity, it would seem more desirable to use additional exchequer funds to raise the maintenance grant for students from disadvantaged backgrounds.

Thus far we have reviewed some initiatives which might assist a greater proportion of students from disadvantaged backgrounds to qualify for higher education places and subsequently to be able to take up these places. An alternative strategy is to accept the reality that because of marked differences in family resources, students from disadvantaged backgrounds cannot compete on an equal footing and that the best way to move towards equality of participation is to establish a quota of places for such students. The idea of a quota is not new: at present most colleges have a special quota for mature students. Some have a quota for overseas and other special category students. Many continental countries, where a *numerus clausus* exists, have separate competitions for places for students coming from different types of post-primary schools.

The idea of a pool of reserved places for students from disadvantaged backgrounds was first raised in the Technical Working Group report and endorsed by the Steering Committee on the Future Development of Higher Education. The scheme envisaged that there would be alternative, and less competitive, entry requirements for these places with, where appropriate, success in a special access programme a prerequi-

site to securing a place. It was envisaged that the pool of reserved places would represent about 2 per cent of total entrants and that, ideally, this should be done in the context of a
planned expansion in provision, thus maximising the accept-
ability of the "quota". This latter consideration is not a trivial
one in view of the range of legal challenges which have been
brought against affirmative action policies in the United
States.

It is too early to assess what the level of implementation has
been, nationally, in respect of the proposal for a pool of reserved places for students from disadvantaged backgrounds.
University College Dublin has put in place such a scheme, although it has not yet achieved the level of take-up which would
meet the two per cent target. Individual faculties have been
free to set the minimum points requirement for their own
courses. In this context there has been a concern among some
academic staff about whether students admitted under this
scheme will be able to meet the academic requirements of the
course. This raises the question of a possible need for dedicated
"access" or preparatory programmes which would ensure an
adequate academic preparation. In addition, third-level institutions need to put in place the necessary tutorial and other support structures which assist students in adapting to the demands of higher education. The need for support structures
extend beyond purely academic considerations. An important
issue which arises in the context of students from lower working class backgrounds (whether school leavers or mature students) participating in higher education is the cultural discon-
tinuity between the family and community experiences of the
student and the essentially middle class ethos of third-level
institutions, especially universities. It is essential that the staff
of third-level institutions become conscious of the "social distance" experienced by working class students and that appro-

priate support structures be provided to combat feelings of alienation.

Perhaps the most over-riding requirement for a successful programme to combat disadvantage is the development of a co-ordinated policy at institutional, community and national level. Higher education institutions should be required to define their objectives, strategies and policies for achieving greater equality with regard to the composition of the student population. Institutions should also be required to review their current procedures with a view to identifying and removing any barriers to entry. Clearly a proactive stance is essential if the representation of those from disadvantaged backgrounds is to be increased. In this context it seems essential that a policy for wider access should be formally adopted by governing bodies and set within the institutional mission statement. Perhaps the best and earliest example of this is to be found in Australia. However, the Universities Act, 1997, provides a statutory basis for this policy in Ireland.

The policies of institutions must, of course, be supported by clearly defined national policies in this area and by a commitment to provide the necessary financial support for the initiatives taken. The linking of additional discretionary funding to colleges in respect of approved intervention programmes represents an important leverage for change.

A third desirable element is the involvement of community groups and activists working in areas of disadvantage. Optimum results will be achieved when local communities endorse the policy initiatives taken as their policies with which they can fully identify.

Conclusion

In conclusion, it is clear that the level of inequality in access to higher education presents a serious challenge to public policy.

There is no simple panacea which will eliminate inequalities. However, if there is a political will to take well designed and co-ordinated action substantial progress can be made. This intervention cannot be confined to the education system alone. In this context it is of interest to note the findings of comparative research which suggests that in Sweden and Netherlands — the two countries which appear to have achieved most success in this area — the relatively greater reduction in inequality is associated with a general policy of equalisation of socio-economic conditions in these countries (Shavit and Blossfeld, 1993). Perhaps the greatest fear is that any society might seek scapegoats as a justification for inaction. The widespread popularity of Herrnstein and Murray's book *The Bell Curve*, in the United States provides such an example. Herrnstein and Murray argued persuasively that it is a person's innate intelligence which determines their life chances, well-being and social position, and (more importantly) that nothing can be done about it. However, as against this pessimism, we should note the important analysis of a group of Berkeley sociologists who offered an outstanding refutation of the Bell Curve thesis. Claude Fischer and his colleagues put the situation in perspective when they point out that if all adults in the United States had the same IQ score but different family backgrounds and environments (as at present), income inequality would decrease by about 10 per cent. In contrast, if all adults had the same family origins and environments but had different IQ scores (as at present), income inequality would decrease by about 37 per cent. While it will never be possible to achieve an equalisation of environments, we do have a responsibility to reduce gross inequalities in circumstances and to try to compensate, through the educational system, those who come from seriously disadvantaged backgrounds.

References

Callan, T. and Harman, C. (1997), *The Economic Returns to Schooling in Ireland* working paper, WP 97/23, Dublin: UCD, Centre for Economic Research.

Callan, T., C. O'Donoghue and C. O'Neill (1994), *Analysis of Basic Income Schemes for Ireland*, Dublin: The Economic and Social Research Institute, Policy Research Series Paper No.21.

Clancy, P. (1995), *Access to College: Patterns of Continuity and Change*: Dublin, Higher Education Authority.

Fischer, C.S. et al. (1996), *Inequality by Design: Cracking the Bell Curve Myth*, Princeton, NJ: Princeton University Press.

Herrnstein, R. and Murray, C. (1994), *The Bell Curve: Intelligence and Class Structure in the United States*, New York: The Free Press.

Investment in Education (1966), Report of the Survey Team Appointed by the Minister for Education, Dublin: Stationery Office.

OECD (1997), *Education at a Glance: OECD Indicators*, Paris: OECD.

Shavit, Y. and Blossfeld, H.P. (eds.) (1993), Persistent Inequality: Changing Educational Attainment in Thirteen Countries, Boulder CO: Westview Press.

Steering Committee on the Future Development of Higher Education (1995), *Report*, Dublin: Higher Education Authority.

Technical Working Group (1995), *Interim Report of the Steering Committee's Technical Working Group*, Dublin: Higher Education Authority.

13

Higher Education — Who Benefits from its Development?

Séamus Puirséil

Irish higher education faces more major changes following its remarkable five-fold rise in enrolments since 1970, the year the first five Regional Technical Colleges opened.

The transformation will mark the early part of the new millennium, just as dramatic expansion marked the last 30 years of the old one. Change will come from a variety of forces — the social and economic case for greater adult participation and second-chance education, changing student demographics and advances in technology as a teaching and learning tool.

Oxford University's decision to start offering degree courses over the Internet refocused interest in the commercial implications of the Internet and the opportunities it now presents.

Irish higher level institutions have recognised the Internet's potential as a learning aid and some are already exploiting the technology as an educational tool. In one institution, for instance, a database module of a computer applications degree course is delivered completely over the Internet. Students download audio lectures synchronised with visual course material appearing on their web browsers. Lectures feature a search facility and index to material where students can play back areas of the course where the topic in question was discussed.

Tutorial sections of the course allow students to meet online to discuss course material, follow set exercises and clarify course content.

Online education has been identified as a useful vehicle for postgraduate and distance learning. Offering courses through community centres and libraries can also reach communities which traditionally have not benefited from higher education.

The opportunities opened up by the new technology for people living in remote or inaccessible situations should also appeal to college administrators, particularly in the area of adult education, with potential savings on sending out teachers to remote areas. There is also the potential for importing and exporting specific skills online, with Irish colleges having the opportunity to play to their own strengths in areas of specialisation.

If the likes of Harvard, Stanford, MIT and Cambridge use their resources to compete in the global academic market, it could create difficulty for smaller colleges. Irish higher level institutions would need to find niche markets, such as Irish Studies, and market them globally.

Irish higher education is well represented in a project, *Technology Foresight* (1999), which aims to anticipate the likely technological advances by 2015. Eight panels of experts looked at a range of sectors, including computer hardware, software and telecommunications technology; natural resources; chemicals and pharmaceuticals, health and life sciences; construction and infrastructure; materials and manufacturing processes; transport and logistics; and energy.

Such foresight activity already exists within the Government agency Forfás, which advises and co-ordinates efforts in industrial development, science and technology. Technology Foresight, under the control of the Irish Council for Science, Technology and Innovation, benefits, however, from having a membership drawn from outside of State agencies. It also has the freedom to apply a broad-based approach as it hopefully raises the right questions on Ireland's future and draws conclusions on the action needed to enhance its national technological capabilities to meet future needs. Forfás supplied an invaluable support network to the Technology Foresight project.

This process of long-term thinking and planning has been shown to be highly successful in some of the world's most developed economies. The report should help as a guide to course planning in higher education, the areas needing special emphasis and, of course, R & D.

A concern for all higher level institutions is the cost implications of developing and delivering courses electronically, as online education requires constant technical development and support. A collaborative approach where students can register with individual institutions, but the technical delivery and management of the courses would be a joint enterprise, could be helpful in this respect.

At undergraduate level, the main impact of new technology is likely to be on how the process is managed. For instance, it would release staff from tedious repetitive teaching for interaction and discussion with students.

The issues of equality of access and participation together with the obvious need to greatly increase the numbers of adults and second-chance education provision are the most formidable challenges facing the higher education system in the years ahead. Educational inequalities are most glaring at higher level and in the open, pluralistic and media-influenced society of our times they are likely to become even more controversial.

Using 1995 per capita costs for different levels of education, the £11,400 spent by the education system on a child who leaves after primary school and the £15,850 incurred on behalf of a child who leaves after two years of secondary school, is in sharp contrast to the £37,525 spent by the State on behalf of a student who completes a four-year programme at third level. This latter figure does not include the full effect of the abolition of fees in 1995.

Ireland's unique demographic situation in recent years, with almost half of its population under 25 years, caused a soaring demand by school-leavers for third-level places. Unfortunately, the proportion of students over the age of 25 in Irish higher education in 1995 was considerably less than the average for all OECD countries.

In Ireland, the percentage of the population of those aged between 25 and 34 years who had completed at least upper secondary education was three points behind the average for the EU and seven points below the average for the OECD, according to 1995 data. For the 25 to 64-year-old age group, the corresponding percentage in the Irish population was only 47 per cent, which was considerably below the averages for the EU and the OECD. However, Ireland has more technology graduates in this age group than any other country.

That rather disappointing 47 per cent figure reflects the fact that in the immediate post-war years all of Northern Europe, with the exception of Ireland, made major changes in their educational systems. Following the publication of *Investment in Education* in 1966, free second-level education was introduced in 1967.

Many of the other countries of Northern Europe, which invested heavily in education in the immediate post-war years, saw rapid rates of economic growth up to and including the 1970s. The slow-down in growth in Europe in the 1980s and the 1990s partly reflects the fact that the major dividend from increased educational investment had already been reaped. By contrast, Ireland began 20 years late and is seeing the benefits of the investment 20 years after its Northern European counterparts. Despite evidence of considerable progress in closing the gaps, the overall attainment levels of our population of working age would still be below the EU and OECD averages by the year 2015 unless we continue to improve our participation and completion rates.

There is now a consensus among economists that investment in education and training is at least as important as investment in buildings, plant, equipment and other physical infrastructure in determining long-term economic growth. Our economic growth rates averaged over 7.5 per cent in the last five years. At the heart of this success have been the skills of our people. The extension of second-level education and the creation of the Regional Technical Colleges were two major decisions which provided the foundations on which we have built the growth of the last ten years.

The Higher Education Authority (HEA) and the National Council for Educational Awards (NCEA) have played pivotal roles in the development of our higher education system. The HEA was set up in 1968 and four years later the NCEA was established to ensure that third-level institutions, outside the universities, maintain appropriate national and international standards and keep pace with technological and industrial advancement. The NCEA was established on a statutory basis in 1980 under the NCEA Act of 1979, with additional responsibility for the overall development and co-ordination of higher education outside of the universities.

In its first year, 1972, the NCEA awarded 51 National Certificates. Last year, it conferred more than 15,000 awards at National Certificate, National Diploma, Degree and Postgraduate levels, bringing the total number of awards to date to approximately 155,000. These figures indicate the dramatic development and expansion achieved by the partnership between the NCEA and its more than 40 designated institutions. The framework of NCEA awards links the network of institutions and their courses together and provides excellent educational opportunities for school-leavers, adult learners, full-time and part-time students.

The Institutes of Technology (formerly the Regional Technical Colleges) will have the opportunity to build on their positive standing in the coming years and to continue to provide a major impetus to the creation of a high-skills base and regional development. The Minister for Education and Science, Micheál Martin TD, has promised that the technological sector will be the major beneficiary of the £250 million Scientific and Technological Education Investment Fund established by the Government.

One of the current challenges facing higher education is to meet the skill shortages that have developed in certain sectors of the economy. The Expert Group on Future Skills Needs, chaired by Dr Chris Horn, and the Task Force on Supply of Technicians to the Irish Economy, chaired by Dr Sean McDonagh, are addressing the problem. If we can get our skills forecasts correct and continue to plan our educational and training output to deliver the required skills, Ireland will have achieved a major competitive advantage.

Future enrolment trends in higher education and the composition of the student body could be crucially important in the new millennium. Despite a five-fold increase in enrolments since 1970 to well over 100,000 at present, Ireland's participation rate has lagged behind that in most other European countries. Currently, approximately 65 per cent of Leaving Certificate students enrol in third-level education, broadly defined.

Past projections of participation have tended to be overtaken in reality. The Green Paper (1992) figure of 100,000 full-time students for the year 2000 has already been exceeded. At the National Education Convention (1994) the Department of Education raised its projections to 115,000 by 2000 with a further growth to 122,000 by 2005. The report of the HEA Technical

Working Group in 1995 projected a figure of 111,500 for 2000, rising to 125,400 by 2010.

The HEA Steering Committee's projections were more modest than those of the Technical Working Group and ranged from 112,000 in 2000, to 119,000 in 2005 and 120,000 in 2010. The representative of the Department of Finance was unable to agree with these figures, regarding them as too high. In February 1997, at the instigation of the Department of Finance, the Government appointed a new committee, with strong representation from government departments, to prepare new projections for of all post-secondary education, including higher education.

According to a Cabinet memorandum, obtained under the Freedom of Information Act, Charlie McCreevy TD, Minister for Finance, pointed out that the number of 18-year-olds would start to drop in 1998.

However, some believe that the numbers of returning emigrants will affect demographic projections and they point to the need to cater for a more diverse student profile in higher education. Another recession, of course, could seriously affect projections. It is interesting to recall that even in the 1980s, when many other sectors suffered severe cutbacks, the education system was considered to have received privileged treatment. In fact, the rise in participation rates since 1980 has been even greater than that which occurred under the first 15 years of the free education policy.

The result has been a radical change in the educational attainment of the adult population over the course of a single generation. In addition, the quality of the intake of students is at its highest level ever and the percentage of students graduating with honours from degree-level programmes increased from 30 per cent in 1965 to 72 per cent in 1992. Irish graduate students tend to achieve very well in postgraduate courses in well-regarded international universities. International employers also seem impressed by the quality of Irish graduates.

A broad range of benefits, both public and private, economic and social, is related to investment in higher education. Some of the public economic benefits include increased tax revenues — individuals with higher levels of education generally contribute more to the tax base as a result of their higher earnings.

Another benefit is greater productivity — although American productivity has increased only modestly in the last two decades, nearly all of that increase has been attributed to the overall increased education level of the workforce.

Studies indicate that the overall growth in consumption in the last four decades is associated with the increasing education levels of society, even after controlling for income.

Higher education contributes to workforce flexibility by educating individuals in generalisable skills — critical thinking, writing, and interpersonal communication, each essential for economic competitiveness.

Understandably, perhaps, the private economic benefits of higher education have tended to attract more interest. In Ireland, the Dale Tussing Report on educational expenditure, published in 1978, focused on the private and public benefits of education, using the former to justify proposed tuition fee payments by the better off. The same arguments were later advanced in support of a graduate tax. In 1993, the Report of the Advisory Committee on Third-Level Student Support highlighted the private benefits of third-level education. It proposed abolition of covenant relief, that the means test for third-level grants should comprise both an income test and a capital test and that savings should be used to increase expenditure under the students grants scheme. However, the Government's response was the abolition of third-level tuition fees.

As a result of their higher levels of education, individuals earn higher salaries and benefits — in both lifetime and average income terms. Surveys indicate that those with a bachelor's degree or higher have greater interest-earning assets, home equity and other financial assets. People who have attended college tend to work more in white-collar jobs, with better conditions and conveniences, ranging from computers to on-site childcare. Research indicates that the ability to change jobs, or to relocate, is correlated with educational attainment.

There are also many public social benefits associated with higher education, while private social benefits include improved health-life expectancy, improved quality of life for offspring, better consumer decision-making, increased personal status, and more hobbies and leisure activities.

The projected fall in school-leaver numbers will provide a precious opportunity to redress our traditional inequalities and imbalances at third level.

14

What Kind of Change
for Universities?

Daniel O'Hare

I wish to honour Michael Enright by taking a tentative look at the future, from the particular perspective of university education. My object is not to indulge in forecasting the form the future will take, but rather to discuss how we might approach some of the challenges which the first part of the next millennium will pose for the people of Ireland.

We have already in this country moved to a situation in which the education system is in constant evolution. The closing 40 years of this century have seen massive change at all levels of the system, change on a scale that most people in the 1950s would have considered to be quite outside the realms of practical possibility.

But before we congratulate ourselves unduly on that achievement, it is well to remember that all this change has been evolutionary both in nature and indeed in pace. We have certainly shifted the scenery, but do we have the capability to change the plot? Will our undoubted ability to change slowly be adequate as a response to an outside environment that will be fundamentally different to what has gone before?

These questions are especially relevant to universities. Because of their nature and the way they are organised, they are not disposed to think very much about fundamental change. In contrast, I believe they have in this century shown themselves to be rather good at incremental change. Allied to the search for knowledge for which universities are perhaps best known is a parallel search for constant improvement.

That search is driven by three forces:

- First is the simple passion to improve — an offshoot of the pride any worker takes in their craft.

- Second is the force of opportunity — created by the fact that as new tools become available to us, we seek to exploit them to the full. Currently, this applies most pervasively to the tools of information technology, which are opening up new possibilities in teaching and learning just as exciting as in any other field.

- Third is the force of demand. The environment in which learning takes place is changing fast — in social terms, in economic terms, in technological terms. This puts new demands on the world of learning — and responding effectively to them is a powerful impetus to improvement.

The combination of these forces has created an improvement agenda that is as long as it is detailed, and it has firmly engaged the energies of university people in Ireland as it has elsewhere. But will improvement be enough? I am prompted to wonder about this because of the fundamental nature of the changes we are beginning to see in the environment that impinges on university education.

Without claiming to be exhaustive, I will look at this landscape of change from four separate perspectives.

First Change: Universities Must Now be for All
This change has not yet taken place: universal access to university education is not already a fact. But increasingly it is

recognised as a right that is on its way to inevitable realisation. Throughout their history, universities have been centres for an elite. Now they must accommodate all.

When I say centres for an elite, I am not talking about an intellectual elite but a social one. Academics might want to defend the notion of catering to an intellectual elite, but the historical reality is that universities have never done so. What they have done is catered for the well-off section of society, and ignored the rest.

What we are talking about now is removing the element of social exclusion that has always been a part of university tradition, though not a part we university people tend to harp on very much. It is now almost the conventional wisdom that the university of the 21st century must be a university for all, blind to the socio-economic background of its students. But making that happen raises issues that go far beyond the brute physical details of bricks, mortar and cash.

For instance, there is the need to provide learning in ways that are fully accessible to a universal student population. Up to now, universities could restrict their entry to people who had shown themselves skilled in a particular way of learning — a way that is perfectly legitimate but one that is not suited to everyone's abilities. People learn in different ways, but universities do not yet reflect the full spectrum of those ways. Our tradition has been based on a particular methodology of learning, rather than on a focus on intellectual capacity per se.

We have assumed that universities can concentrate exclusively on "academic" methods and standards, and some would argue that this is precisely a university's job. However, while we can certainly open an academic university to everyone without changing it, we cannot in such an unchanged environment help everyone to realise their full potential. We would be condemning a significant number of students to a second-class existence and a second-class experience.

But opening up the university so that it recognises a far broader range of talents and achievements, daunting as it is, is only part of the challenge. The university must do this while maintaining its reputation as the ultimate fount of excellence in the community's asset base of knowledge and innovation. For a university to turn its back on excellence would be to turn its back on a necessary part of its essence.

I am not suggesting, as people sometimes unwisely do, that everything and everybody in every university is excellent. But universities have succeeded in creating the possibility of excellence, and it seems to me vital that this element must be preserved.

Is the notion of a "haven for excellence" compatible with the notion of universal access? Is it possible for a single institution to achieve both aims?

If it is not, then we would need to contemplate two quite different institutions — each focusing on one of the aims. Such an outcome would, in my view, lose much of the university ideal. I believe that both objectives are attainable within the same organisation if we set our minds to doing so.

I particularly resist the view that achieving universal access must inevitably involve a process of "dumbing down". After all, in their traditional role of catering for the well-off, universities have always accommodated both the brilliant and the not so brilliant — perhaps not indeed in equal numbers. The concept of mixed abilities is certainly not new.

But the tension between universal access and the university as a fount of excellence is a real one, in practical terms. The move to a universal university is a fundamental change that must be addressed.

Second Change: The State is Now the University's Main Patron

Increasingly across the world, the university's dominant paymaster is the State.

Private universities do not escape this trend, even in the United States; they rely heavily on State income, both from scholarships to individual students and even more from government research contracts. Neither will the growing pressure to supplement the funding of public universities with private donations reduce the State involvement below the level of dominance.

The tensions created by this are obvious. What is taught, and how it is taught, becomes a matter in which the State has a legitimate interest. It would be foolish for university people to claim that the State's interest is illegitimate per se; the issue is how, and on what basis, it is to be limited.

This is far from a theoretical issue. We have already seen here in Ireland that as it assumes more of the payment burden, the State tends to move beyond a generalised feeling that all education is a good thing. The State becomes more and more specific in the tunes it wishes to pay the piper for.

Disciplines with immediate relevance to the national economy tend to be favoured, while disciplines with no obvious relevance find it harder to gain favour.

A particular danger here is that some disciplines which are at the very heart of a university's mission, in particular those that encourage independent thought and speculation, may be regarded by the State as lacking in priority — or even as subversive. Independent, critical thought in general may be less valued than the simple acquisition of skills that are readily marketable in the economic marketplace. Departments of Philosophy in smaller universities, as was shown in the UK in the 1980s, may find it difficult even to survive.

Both State and universities have typically so far failed to re-solve this issue at the level of principle, confining their efforts to annual skirmishes over spending allocations. Can we create a model which would properly reflect the State's dominant role as paymaster, while allowing a university enough space and freedom to pursue its own agenda of priorities?

I believe such a model is possible. It must, however, be based on an acceptance by society that the value of universities is wider than a purely economic one, and the reality is that at present society in general does not hold that view. It is up to universities to develop and present that model, and work to persuade society to adopt it.

The fact that we in the university community have so far conspicuously failed to do this is all the more remarkable, given that time is not on our side but on the side of the State. The State can, and often does, get its way by attrition over a succession of spending cycles.

Third Change: The University's Walls No Longer Have a Function

Fundamental to the old concept of the university was its sepa-ration from the rest of the world — symbolised by the high walls that traditionally bounded its campus.

Learning took place apart, and learning was conceived as a self-contained entity that was then carried into the outside world as a package by graduating students. Academics were often content merely to add to the body of knowledge, without feeling any compulsion to bring the good news to those outside the walls.

Equally, the inner walls between university disciplines were long regarded as load-bearing structural divisions rather than partitions of convenience.

These walls, whether internal or external, are no longer relevant to today's needs. Within the university, some of the most exciting developments take place where discipline boundaries meet and where they overlap. This is not incidental, it is systemic; and it illustrates how boundaries between disciplines can inhibit rather than encourage the progress of knowledge.

Another internal boundary is between research and undergraduate teaching. With the body of knowledge changing so fast, the distinction between the two is becoming increasingly blurred. The need is to integrate them wherever possible. It may well be time to junk the traditional structure of disciplines altogether, in order to exploit the full potential of future exploration of the boundaries of knowledge.

Between the university and the outside world, walls are also now becoming a hindrance rather than a support to the academic agenda. Look at what is happening:

- Work experience is now widely seen as integral to the learning process. The aim is not to prepare students for working life, though that is a valuable by-product. The real purpose is to draw closer together the worlds of theory and practice, and to produce graduates who are at home in both those worlds.

- The boundary between university research and entrepreneurial activity is becoming meaningless. The value of campus enterprises is in pursuing the notion of knowledge as a seamless web that carries all the way to application in the real world.

- Today's university is less and less an inward-looking repository of knowledge than an outward-looking portal to an entire world of information, accessed instantly through telecommunications. Increasingly, that portal serves not just the university itself but a wider community.

- Above all, learning need no longer take place physically within the walls. With distance learning, the umbilical cord between the learning process and the student's physical presence on the university campus can finally be broken.

Yet we still have our walls. So far we have done nothing more than chip away at a brick or two. At best, we have replaced some of them with tasteful hedges. Is there a need — I suggest there is — for a more fundamental demolition job? Is there a need for a university structure that properly reflects the new needs and the new possibilities? A university without walls, either internal or external — or indeed, without the walls we build so readily in our own minds?

Fourth Change: The Time-frame Has Shifted

Traditionally, universities as teaching institutions have been conceived as "upfront loaders". Students came directly from school, got their packet of knowledge, and departed into adult life to apply it.

In recent years, we have tinkered around the edges of this conception of the university. We have increased the number of mature students, and their proportion of the study body. We have put more resources into distance learning. In doing so we provide people with a second chance to access a university education. We also make a genuflection to the notion of lifetime learning. But our universities are still structured so that these changes are merely side-shows to the main event.

We do not need a crystal ball to foresee that the needs catered for in this way will grow at an extremely fast rate. What happens to universities when these needs become mainstream?

What happens when it becomes the exception, rather than the rule, to go direct from school to university? When it becomes exceptional to pursue study in one continuous stream, and more the norm to do so in instalments — either in between or in tandem with pursuing a career? Will we, I wonder, still organise our universities to cater for a norm that no longer applies?

In addressing all these different types of change, the generic challenge is the same: *can universities evolve satisfactorily to meet the new situation?* Or do we at some stage need to re-invent the organisation in a radical sense?

From this perspective, we need to ask:

- What, in the most fundamental sense, are universities trying to do?

- In responding to the myriad changes in our environment, are universities staying true to the core reasons for their very existence?

- Do they need to find new ways, and new structures, to serve those reasons in the future?

- Do they even need to find new reasons for their existence, to reflect fully the era in which we live?

- Do universities, as we traditionally know them, have any useful future at all?

- Is the best way forward to evolve from what we have now? Or is it to discard that model and create a totally new one for the radically different conditions the world faces now?

- If the university did not already exist, and we had to create an organisation to fill the post-schooling need, would we invent the kind of university we know today?

In seeking answers to these and other similar questions, I believe we must look to our values. I see academic values as a guiding beacon in a sea of change.

What *are* the fundamental values that drive us? There are times when we need to examine and perhaps question our basic assumptions, and I suggest there was never a greater need to do so than now, against the landscape of change I have been sketching above.

Let me therefore conclude by putting forward my own modest shopping list of values, in the hope that it may provoke discussion. Not surprisingly, I don't have any new values to add — but I do believe that some of our accepted values need revisiting.

1. Traditionally, academic values begin with a genuflection to the god of knowledge. For instance, the pursuit of knowledge for its own sake. I have to say I think this approach accounts for a large chunk of one of the walls between the university and the wider world that I would be happy to destroy.

   Instead, I suggest that in today's circumstances the fundamental task is not the pursuit of knowledge but rather *the development of critical minds*. That is surely our real role, both as teachers and researchers — helping to develop the minds of others, and developing our own critical faculties as a life-long pursuit. Produce the critical minds and the pursuit of knowledge will flow automatically.

2. Second, I would place the commitment to *push back the frontiers of knowledge,* and to share the resulting product widely. Many people in this world, particularly those of the paymaster variety, are concerned only with what already exists. In practical terms, they have a view of knowledge and human potentiality which is essentially static. This leads to a wish to conceive educational institutions merely as caretakers of the books, as passers-along of the supposed tablets of stone, and as certifiers of accredited skills.

It is a fundamental academic value, and a value under threat, that knowledge is dynamic and open-ended. If we wish to preserve this value, we must accept a twin commitment that goes with the drive to extend knowledge. We must accept it is also our responsibility to communicate our progress to the wider world. We must throw aside the notion that our responsibility stops with the production of knowledge itself. As new knowledge becomes more complex and difficult to understand by outsiders, it becomes in my view a major responsibility of the inner circle to communicate its knowledge outwards in terms that are accessible outside.

3. Third, and perhaps surprisingly to some, I suggest it is now a desirable academic value to be an *engine of economic growth and development*. Academics have always been somewhat shy of "relevance", the way old-style aristocrats used to turn up their noses at anything smacking of "trade". I suggest it should become part of our thinking that making an economic contribution is a fundamental part of our activity, rather than a pragmatic or utilitarian response. It is not by any means all we do, but it is a part of it.

4. Fourth, I suggest it is a basic academic value to be, in a central and meaningful sense, *the conscience of society*. The university should be, should be seen to be, and should be *expected* to be, the primary institution which constantly queries the assumptions of society. Not alone that, the university should also be a primary resource for providing society with a range of alternative options to pursue. As a centre of criticism, it should be constructive. And where appropriate, the university in its own actions should provide society with a lead.

No area of activity or of thought should be off-limits in this regard. The university's constructive questioning role should extend to politics, to ethics, to social organisation and income distribution, to the myriad issues around freedom, equality, and human rights. I believe this activist, pathfinder role should be seen by all academics as fundamental to the university's role, not one that is engaged in peripherally or occasionally.

5. The concept of the university as society's conscience brings me to my final value, which is *autonomy*. The notion of academic autonomy has been much abused by university people. It is perhaps time to clean off some of the moss that has gathered on the concept with the passage of time.

Why is academic autonomy necessary at all? In my view, it is entirely bound up with the role of being the conscience of society. If universities do not pursue that role, they have no justification to claim autonomy. But if universities do fulfil that role, it goes without saying that to pursue it effectively they must be genuinely independent of the pressures within society.

Universities should not muzzle themselves because they are afraid of offending the powers that be. They should not tailor what they have to say to the agenda of their paymasters. It seems superfluous to point this out. And yet, when we look around and when we listen, what is surely remarkable in this last part of the twentieth century is the virtual silence of academics.

Have universities, and the academics within them, already largely abdicated their role as the conscience of society? If so, I suggest that it is a matter of urgency for them to rediscover it. For if they do not do so, the most prized traditional academic value of all — autonomy — will cease to have a solid justification.

In summary, it is my belief that a fundamentally changing external environment for Irish universities will demand that their response is fundamental rather than incremental. In seeking to find a way down that road of change, I believe our best starting-point is to re-examine our values from first principles.

15

Green Light for a Learning Society?
The Green Paper "Adult Education in
an Era of Lifelong Learning"

Kevin Hurley

Rationale for the Learning Society

Taking "learning" as that which is pursued within a systematic framework, a learning society can be said to be one in which opportunities for access and participation are lifelong and lifewide and distributed equitably throughout the subsisting community. It values and fosters not only early childhood education, compulsory education, and post-compulsory initial education and training but, also, all forms of post-initial education and training. At the post-initial — and least developed — stage it embraces a diversity of activity differentiated by function and context quite apart from nomenclature (such as adult education, adult training, continuing education, continuing professional development, in-service education and training, and the less familiar recurrent education, and education permanente). Regardless of designation, function and context, a learning society values and facilitates learning over the life cycle and throughout all constituent sectors.

Schuller puts it well in noting that "as a general aspiration, the learning society is suspiciously unchallengeable". And in this, perhaps, lies a problem for the notion. In the absence of a thorough critique it can be relegated to the zone of worthy projects to be re-visited, perhaps, when other priorities have been discharged. That is like leaving the storm-damaged roof of your house until some journeyman chances along the way. The learning society is not a mere pious aspiration but strategically vital to the future well-being of its constituency.

In Ireland, systematic learning, as it is organised at present, caters almost exclusively for those in the age range 4–21. And on the face of it this provision would seem to be adequate for the emergence of an equable society as outcome. After all it is the aim of primary education to:

> (i) enable children to live full lives as children, (ii) equip them to avail themselves of further education, (iii) prepare them to live full and useful lives as adults in society (Primary School Curriculum Handbooks, 1971, Part I, p. 12).

The Junior Cycle aims to build on this and — paraphrasing drastically — develop personal, social, moral, spiritual and civic capacities in preparation for further education or employment and the fullest exercise of responsible citizenship. Senior cycle education aims to continue this process while also aspiring to develop in the young person a capacity for self-directed learning and for independent thought. Within the initial system the process reaches its apex in higher education. Under the most recent legislation in this sector — the Universities Act, 1997 — universities are charged with eleven objects. Among these are:

- To promote learning in its student body and in society generally;

- To promote the cultural and social life of society;

- To educate, train and retrain higher level professional technical and managerial personnel;

- To facilitate lifelong learning through the provision of adult and continuing education.

It would therefore seem as if, through initial education, adequate provision is being made for sustaining the general good of our society. But that is to acquiesce in the fact that too many students do not complete senior cycle and the majority still do not enter higher education. It also disregards the force of the dynamics that are contributing to accelerated change in the fabric and composition of society and to considerable turbulence in its collective psyche.

Notwithstanding progress, here in Ireland a range of issues pose challenges to the possibility of general equanimity. Among these are the sharp rise in population (despite a decline in fertility), the increase in marriage breakdown, higher levels of extra-marital births, unbalanced urbanisation and nuclearisation, a flight from farming compounding rural depopulation, accelerated growth in the economy cheek-by-jowl with gross inequality in the distribution of wealth, skill shortfalls, the demise of erstwhile authority models to the accompaniment of deepening disenchantment with representational democracy. There is a lot to be learnt by all sectors of society if self is to be congenially grounded in the contemporary world.

A little-noticed, EU-wide survey (Euro Delphi Survey) conducted some years ago provided a notable insight into such challenges but also to the potential for their amelioration by adult education. Presented with 22 "major life problems" the participating Irish learners rank-ordered them as follows (left-hand column). The right-hand column shows how the same group rank-ordered the potential of adult education for the amelioration of these problems:

Major Life Problems	Problems which can be Ameliorated by Adult Education
Unemployment and social inequality	Inaccessibility of new technology
Distrust and ignorance of politics	Unemployment and social inequality
Material poverty	Personal identity
Other forms of social inequality	Access to information
Inaccessibility of new technology	Lack of meaning to life
Limited participation in democracy	Material poverty
Access to information	Distrust and ignorance of politics
Problems of physical mobility	Limited participation in democracy
Lack of meaning to life	Other social inequalities

On the one hand it is reassuring that integrity in politics is an issue of such moment to the adult audience while being forced to conclude that recent events (disclosures at the Flood and Moriarty Tribunals) are likely to have done little to allay distrust. Policy makers should note the findings. Adult education is not merely seen in utility terms — conferring opportunities for access to new technology and employment. More enduringly, it has the potential to help us reflect on our own unique personas and on the conditions within which the same are required to operate. It can also equip us to exert influence on the latter.

The European Commission, in its White Paper on Teaching and Learning, "Towards the Learning Society", further identified three "factors of upheaval" which serve to compound domestic adversity. These are "the internationalisation of trade, the dawning of the information society and the relentless march of science and technology". It concluded that building the learning society entailed such actions as the acquisition of new knowledge, bringing schools (sic) and the business sector closer together, combatting exclusion, developing proficiency in three Community languages and treating capital investment and investment in training on an equal basis. That invites a stock-taking exercise.

Ireland's Candidature as a Learning Society

Not many polities qualify as learning societies. Perhaps the foremost are the Scandinavian countries and the US, if one is to judge by the rate of learning activity among adults. But, with educational achievement now featuring as one of the prime indices of good standing, attention is turning universally towards strategic development in lifelong learning.

Our nearest neighbour (and competitor) is picking up the lessons faster than we appear to be. For several years now the UK has been setting and adjusting national targets for education, while New Labour chose to give the phrase lifelong learning mantra-like status, almost obscuring the rose. Most recently, for instance, David Blunkett, its Secretary for State for Education and Employment, has adopted as a target that 28 per cent of the workforce will have a level 4 qualification (degree or NVQ equivalent) by the year 2002, a modification of an earlier target of 30 per cent, by 2000. A major plank in the strategy to reach this is the participation of mature students in higher education. As a result, mature students now make up more than 30 per cent of those attending university, contrasting with Ireland's derisory 5 per cent. Other targets are:

- 60 per cent of the workforce to be qualified to 2 GCE A level or equivalent

- 70 per cent of all organisations with 200 or more employees, and 35 per cent of those employing 50 or more, to be recognised as Investors in People.

Indeed, there is little evidence of such targeting in Ireland. That target which has been announced is confined to completion rates in the Leaving Certificate and, with the exception, by and large, of VTOS students, is thereby focused on school-leavers. And targeting of adult learners would seem to be imperative to judge by the extent to which Ireland languishes behind developed countries in the lifelong learning league. OECD tables show us badly trailing in eleventh in a twelve horse race behind Sweden, Switzerland (German), New Zealand, UK, US, Netherlands, Canada, Australia, Switzerland (French), Belgium (Flanders), and propped up only by Poland.

The shortfalls in educational achievement in Ireland have begun to receive considerable media attention of late and, more encouragingly, are being acknowledged by those responsible for policy and strategy. While there have long been studies highlighting under-achievement in Ireland it is invariably the publication of an OECD report that serves as catalyst for development; this pertains today as surely as it did, so notably, in the 1960s. Some recent OECD findings are worth rehearsing:

- In the words of the Minister at the launch of the Green Paper on adult education:

  The OECD International Adult Literacy survey, published in 1997, showed that about 25 per cent of the Irish population were found to score at the lowest literacy level. This is the worst performance of any country surveyed (those already named above), except (again) for Poland. Only about 10 per cent in the Netherlands and 6 per cent in Sweden scored at this level.

- In 1995, 47 per cent of the age group 25–64 had completed at least upper secondary education; the EU had a country mean of 54 per cent, and the OECD 60 per cent

- Because of a comparatively late start, the proportion of graduates in Ireland's population falls critically short of the OECD mean and, despite strong recent growth, is not expected to reach par until 2012.

It is against this unfavourable background, and probably influenced by such findings, that the Green Paper "Adult Education in an Era of Lifelong Learning" was launched on 24 November 1998, perhaps also triggering the odyssey towards a learning society.

The Green Paper

The Green Paper has been universally welcomed by those concerned with adult education, perhaps as much for its symbolic force as for its contents. After all, despite the Murphy and Kenny reports, of 1973 and 1984 respectively, the flow of oxygen has been sluggish to say the least. But the advent of the Green Paper combined with the promise of a White Paper is taken to bode a more secure supply.

Priorities Professed

The authors nail their colours to the mast at the outset, clearly indicating, in the introduction, that social concerns must be foremost in shaping strategies and underpinning investment aimed at the development of adult education. "Addressing poverty and disadvantage" is identified as the first priority, an aspiration that is consistent with general social policy. The theme is continued in the second objective, "promoting equality, competitiveness and employment", which trinity nevertheless throws up some disjunctions; certainly if a competitive ethos is seen to be imperative this would appear to require a far more extensive vision and strategy than that focussed only on inclusion. In the third explicit priority, "supporting community advancement", the social thrust is affirmed while in the fourth, "meeting the challenges of change", competitiveness is re-visited briefly but, otherwise, analysis of change is postponed.

There is a striking correlation between the findings of the Euro Delphi Survey and the priorities adopted. Given the impoverished base upon which building must commence it would be unconscionable to do otherwise than pursue the priorities as identified. However, there may be a danger in pursuing these without adverting to the wider vision of a learning society. Is there a danger, for instance, that a symbiotic, integrated front on adult education and training may be forfeit, together with the synergy that might flow from such concert? Are there not already enough binary arrangements and boundaries in the field of education and training?

The Priorities Reinforced

An overview of the grounds which warrant "investment in adult and community education" is also undertaken near the outset, beginning with the assertion that this is justifiable not only on economic and equality grounds but also on cultural and civic grounds to do with the entire body politic.

Given the parameters, the resultant survey is admirably inclusive. It boldly specifies some seven key concepts underpinning an approach to adult education, risking the charge that others are omitted. Echoes from the Euro Delphi Survey can be heard. The EU's more hard-nosed White Paper is invoked and its three "factors of upheaval", namely, "the internationalisation of trade, the dawning of the information society and the relentless march of science and technology", are rehearsed as imperatives for change and upskilling. Patterns of participation in education, and the links between negative outcomes and poverty, are identified. Indeed, we are again reminded of the incidence and comparative levels of poverty in Ireland. All in all, the assertion that adult education has a key role to play in compensatory, empowering and upgrading processes presents as incontestable.

Reviewing Achievements

A survey of the historical evolution of adult education is instructive, not least because of the paucity of development it exposes. In turn this is reflected in the circumscribed tale to be related in regard to current funding, access strategies, existing structures, support services such as guidance and counselling and the non-accreditation of the fathomless learning that has been accumulated by successive waves of adult learners, increasingly at community level.

The paper acknowledges that "national policy is that, except for the most disadvantaged, part-time education provision should be self-financing". Since by definition this entails most of adult education it is not surprising to encounter the figures which are revealed as constituting public underpinning of adult learning in Ireland. In 1998 these were slightly in excess of £65 million. This out of a total expenditure on education of approximately £2,605,478,000, thus amounting to 2.5 per cent. Indeed the Irish exchequer came under considerably less pressure than this figure implied, as the figure for adult education is inflated by funding tranches which originated in Europe rather than Kildare Street; an example is the VTOS scheme to which £26 million of this applied.

The Paper also reveals the relative disadvantage of adult education in comparison with training. Among a range of training providers FÁS looms largest and appears to have expended £369 million in the same period — 568 per cent of that extended to adult education.

Following this survey the Paper indulges in a prophecy that "the agenda for the future of this expanding sector" will be set by certain issues. These are:

- Ireland's low standing in international tables of literacy

- The lack of structures for systematic investment

- The inflexibility of provision to date

- The restricted avenues for progression to third-level education

- Prioritising investment in adult literacy as a key economic objective

- Expanding provision in adult and second chance education

- Developing outreach strategies targeting those most in need

- Greater investment in infrastructure

- Promoting articulation and coherence between education and training providers.

Priming Offensives

The review done, priorities are identified and recommendations made (in Chapter 4) "as to how developments in addressing adult literacy, poverty, employment and competitive issues, and access to third-level education can be progressed".

While the structure of the chapter tends to dissipate focus it is possible to perceive an overview followed by a set of recommendations. A frank acknowledgement of the high levels of difficulty with literacy experienced by adults, a case for greater integration between education and the world of work, mention of the incidence of early school leaving, a scrutiny of the low level of penetration of higher education by adults and a reference to distance education are used as emplacements for the recommendations which follow.

These are then set out as four aggregate recommendations:

- **Implementation of a National Adult Literacy Programme**. This is to be informed by the experience of pilot initiatives in place since 1998.

- **Introduction of a Back to Education Initiative**. Measures here range from the expansion of VTOS in part-time form to the removal of welfare-related obstacles to participation in learning.

- **Enhancement of a Third-Level Mature Student Access Programme**. A list of desiderata culminates in a recommendation to allocate £1 million "to support institutions" for such innovations as a co-ordinating network of participating colleges; short-term access and orientation programmes; counselling, childcare and mentoring supports; demonstration programmes; and workplace, home and community-based innovations in access.

- **Proposals for Upskilling the Workforce**. Key elements of the strategic framework of the Department of Enterprise, Trade and Employment are rehearsed here. Other measures aired include a proposed Savings and Loan Fund for Education. In general this area is approached tentatively, perhaps betraying residues of the territoriality that is being countered under the Public Service's Strategic Management Initiative.

Thereafter other recommendations relate to the effective implementation of an outreach strategy, measures to provide parity for those with disabilities, capital provision, equality principles, and Irish language and culture. However, the chapter culminates in the enigmatic conclusion:

In this Chapter (sic) the priorities for State investment are:

- Addressing literacy needs

- Providing second chance education for adults with less than upper second-level education

- Putting in place the necessary supports, such as guidance, childcare, and certification arrangements to facilitate access and progression in the context of a seamless transition between the different levels of the system.

Measures to Underpin the Offensives

The remaining sections of the paper deal with Community Education, Accreditation/Certification/Guidance, Training of Adult Educators, and Structures.

A thorough critique of community education is distinguished by a definition that challenges all interested parties to evaluate their existing models and ensure that they translate as approaches rather than systems, and result in the actualisation of such principles as partnership and parity.

The issues of accreditation, certification and guidance are surveyed and result in recommendations to develop — speedily — (i) a national framework of qualifications, (ii) to put in place transparent mechanisms for the accreditation of prior experience and learning and (iii) to establish a national comprehensive system of adult guidance and counselling.

The dearth of opportunities for practitioners to acquire qualifications is recognised and the prospects for professionalising the sector are raised. These prompt recommendations to establish an inter-agency working group to progress the case for the formal recognition of professional qualifications, to establish a Forum for Practitioners of Adult and Community Education, and to develop mechanisms for in-service training.

Structure being the navigable way through which the adult education traffic is to flow, weaknesses stemming from lack of coherence and integration in present arrangements warrant attention. These are cited and the main stakeholders are identified prior to the delineation of a model to fit the 21st century. In the first instance comes the recommendation "that a National Adult Learning Council be established as an Executive Agency of the Department of Education and Science." The partiality for capitals does little to assuage the feeling that this is the wrong starting point and somewhat at variance with the earlier rank-ordering of stakeholders and the notions of parity and partnership which resonate throughout the document. Somehow one feels that those most under-represented in education — and ipso facto most qualified to do so — will effect little influence on this body. Unease is sustained further on encountering the first of the recommended functions, namely "to promote the development of the adult education sector in line with national social and economic needs". Nor is it much allayed by the suggested membership. Acquiescing in the traditional mindset informing membership of such bodies the profile in this case might be described as reasonable, with the exception that there is no evidence as to the weighting to be given to the various stakeholders. One form of weighting is clear, however: the concept of fiscal accountability easily outmasses that of participatory democracy.

Local manifestations of structure will be critical to the enhancement of adult learning. It is perhaps not as ominous as might appear that the phrase "would be chosen" appears in the brief rationale for membership of these. Is it also a mere oversight that no express provision is made for learners? The paper omits to address the thorny question as to what should constitute the spatial unit for each board, presumably in the hope that some kind of consensus will emerge from submissions. If so, at least the democratic impulse is re-asserting itself here.

Otherwise the principles which are proposed for underpinning these are redolent of those canvassed throughout the paper, ironically so.

Towards the Learning Society?

If the learning society is a target worthy of pursuit it is not unpromising to recognise that we in Ireland start from a low base and face a formidable challenge. As the evidence cited above suggests, there appears to be a fairly deeply embedded resistance by adults to the resumption of learning. Nor do employers appear to value training adequately. As is noted in the Green Paper, studies indicate that about 1.5 per cent of payroll is spent on training here whereas best international practice fluctuates between 3 and 5 per cent.

The condition implied by these findings leaves Ireland dangerously vulnerable in an environment in which we are daily subject to the growing pressures wrought by change best exemplified by the onset of the other "age" — the Information Age. Information is assuming such importance as a "commodity" that it has the potential to outstrip any of the more conventional exchange goods. Information technology is the vehicle for its transmission, more often than not instantaneously. Those members of society who are incapable of accessing, managing and refining it through exclusion from the learning pale and its electronic appendages will be increasingly marginalised as the Information Age progresses. The society will be the poorer for this, giving rise, in Field's words, to the "knowledge rich" and the "knowledge poor".

The low levels of activity in adult education and training will not change simply because of discovery. Nor as a result of prescription. As with so many other matters of public concern this is a challenge that calls for a community-wide strategy. The challenge is no less than the reversal of cultural conditioning whereby systematic learning is identified exclusively with school and initial education, and, for those most on the margins, too frequently with failure. It is here that the issue of structure is critical. Learning must be recognised, promoted, resourced and celebrated within both neighbourhood communities and communities of interest. And it is particularly critical that the priorities resonating throughout the Green Paper be maintained in this campaign, in view of Sargent's confirmation of the extent to which post-initial education is dominated by those who most benefitted from initial education.

Thus the conceptualisation of structure should be reversed, commencing at the point of greatest need, involving a process distinguished by hallmarks recurring in the paper, such as equal partnership, participatory democracy, area-based approaches, active participation, inclusive discourse and decision-making. Instead, after boldly positing a "lack of core identity at national level" as the foremost weakness, the strategy favoured appears inspired by the principle of cascade. This is consistent with the general tendency to exercise control at the centre. A model for the third quarter of the current century perhaps rather than for the millennium that is upon us!

What are the prospects for a consensus on what would constitute the learning society? Hardly more of the same? Patchy provision of pre-school education? Primary schools starved of the resources for culturally enriching activity? Contradictions between the dynamic ethos of the Transition Year programmes and the oppressive regimes generated by the conflation of Leaving Certificate and points system? Competition for points-determined third-level places greasing the wheels of the grind industry and ensuring the continuing exclusion of those least equipped to cope? A Black Pig's Dyke between education and training? In respect of adult learners, continuing procrastination in addressing the issues that are capable of making learning truly society-wide? The debate has hardly begun on a proposition that warrants thorough critique. A debate that should take on board Schuller's proposition that although

> human capital's portrayal of education as investment is a powerful one . . . it needs to be complemented by an approach which underlines the recognition that learning is a social activity and depends for its value on its embeddedness within a social framework.

If a learning society is to come about it is profoundly to be hoped that it is not only for expedient reasons such as a real crisis in skill shortages, or the threat of irreversible degrading of the environment, or the reversal of shortcomings exposed by the OECD. There is a danger that such arguments may provide the real spur for the incorporation of a lifelong learning strategy. Such utilitarianism achieves too much for the few and too little for the many, perpetuating inequality. And, without the embedding of participatory democracy, it can easily take hold. In profit-hungry North America, for example, where so many of the distinguishing hallmarks of adult education have been forged, latter-day trends give cause for pause. There, expediency has wrought significant change in the extension work of universities so that "financial pressures have moved (it) towards serving elite, affluent audiences . . . [and] a clear and unmistakable movement towards markets with money has supplanted programming directed toward people who cannot afford high extension fees" (Griffith, 1996).

The signs are propitious that this polity will be distinguished by a more inclusive vision of the learning society. After all, the initial system is increasingly visited by initiatives such as Breaking the Cycle, Home/School Liaison and Higher Education Access Projects, while the Universities Act explicitly charges its constituent institutions to formulate and implement equality policies. Additionally, the public service is being impregnated by the spirit of the National Anti-Poverty Strategy and Ireland echoes other members of the EU by constituting a cabinet committee on inclusion. There is a consistency, therefore, in the principles expounded in the Green Paper which encourages the expectation that the promised White Paper will lead to such clear outlines of an inclusive learning society that all can subscribe to the barn-raising.

References

Carey, Liam et al. (1995), *Euro-Delphi Survey — The Future Goals and Policies of Adult Education in Europe 1995*, Maynooth: Maynooth College.

Centre for Educational Research and Innovation (1997), *Education at a Glance OECD Indicators*, Paris: OECD.

Commission on Adult Education (1983), *Lifelong Learning*, Dublin: Stationery Office.

European Commission (1995), *Teaching and Learning — Towards the Learning Society*, Office for Official Publications of the European Communities, Brussels.

Fender, Brian (1998), *Higher Education Funding for 1999–00 and Beyond*, Department for Education and Employment, Bristol.

Field, John (1998), "The Silent Explosion — Living in the Learning Society" in *Adults Learning*, December, Vol. 10, No. 24, pp. 6–8.

Griffith, William S., (1996), "Communities, Universities and Change: Recent North American Experience" in Elliott, Jane et al., *Communities and Their Universities: The Challenge of Lifelong Learning*, London: Lawerence & Wishart.

Jarvis, Peter (ed.) (1992), *Perspectives on Adult Education and Training in Europe*, Leicester: The National Institute of Adult Continuing Education.

O'Dea, Willie (1998), "Green Paper: Adult Education in an Era of Lifelong Learning", Speaking Note.

Organisation for Economic Co-operation and Development (1997), *Literacy Skills for the Knowledge Society*, Paris: OECD.

Schuller, Tom (1998), "Three Steps Towards a Learning Society" in *Studies in the Education of Adults*, April, Vol. 30, No. 1, pp. 11–20.

Stationery Office, *Universities Act 1997*, Dublin.

Tuckett, Alan (1997), *Lifelong Learning in England and Wales*, Leicester: The National Institute of Adult Continuing Education.

16

Lifelong Learning: The Role of Unions as Knowledge Brokers

Peter Cassells

The idea of lifelong learning has been gaining currency since the 1970s, and more particularly since 1996, which was designated the European Year of Lifelong Learning. This concept is growing in importance in the debates on equity and labour market participation at an Irish and a European level. Yet we still lack either an accurate definition of what precisely constitutes lifelong learning, or a working model suitable for the Irish context.

Role of Unions

The role of unions in this area is of long standing. From the nineteenth century onwards, unions included a worker education element to their activities. This has evolved into a network of semi-autonomous worker education associations in most European countries, and into a wide range of activist education, which has developed from the original shop steward courses. I know of many cases where the first steps towards adult education were taken at a shop stewards course.

Unions also have a natural empathy with the egalitarian assumptions which underlie the lifelong learning debate. Congress was able to put this empathy to practical use in 1991 when, in the course of the negotiations leading to the agreement on the Programme for Economic and Social Progress, Congress secured an agreement to the mainstreaming of the Educational Opportunity scheme into what became VTOS, and to the establishment of 12 area-based companies to combat disadvantage. The effects of these two initiatives are still working their way through Irish society.

Many unions are now approaching lifelong learning from a third perspective. Just as the role of unions as bargainers for wages and conditions was expanded in successive decades to new agendas in areas such as paid holidays and subsequently in the area of health and safety and pensions, as we enter into a knowledge-based society, unions are developing a role as knowledge brokers for members. This role is played by advancing the agenda at national level, by developing partnerships with providers and, to an increasing extent, by directly engaging in job-related education and training for their members.

What is Lifelong Learning?

In 1996, the European Centre for the Development of Vocational Training (CEDEFOP) devoted an entire issue of their journal to lifelong learning, which in the introduction stated that lifelong learning was not a well-defined issue, thus pointing out a weakness at the heart of the debate. The OECD goes further in its most recent work, which states that "the all embracing nature of the concept of lifelong learning could lead to a vagueness (and) loss of focus" (1998). There is, therefore, a real danger that this important debate could collapse under the weight of generalities.

In the Irish context, this means that we urgently need an agreed definition of what lifelong learning means, together with the outline of a working model of a system of lifelong learning. My belief is that the main focus should be on developing a culture of work-based learning.

I am not convinced that measures needed to improve completion rates in the mainstream system are appropriate to the lifelong learning framework. While vitally important to society, they should be located within the local development framework, where they could build on the valuable work already undertaken in this sector.

I suggest, therefore, that in the Irish context lifelong learning can help to resolve the following contradictions:

- Where we combine a high retention rate of the 16–21 age cohort with a rate of second level completion in the 18–64 age group which is one of the lowest in Northern Europe.

- Where we combine an imaginative programme for second chance education at second level (VTOS) with a level of mature student access to university that is very low by European standards.

- Where we fund the third-level education of school leavers and of those from a disadvantaged background, but leave part-time students in work to bear 100 per cent of costs (even though learning for those at work might produce the quickest returns for the economy as a whole).

We might also consider defining what lifelong learning is *not*. It is not simply the "rebranding" of existing education or training programmes. This will be seen by consumers and outside observers alike for what it is — an attempt to put old wine in new bottles. In order to avoid this confusion, I prefer the earlier definition, as applied in the Nordic countries, as "recurrent education". The key focus of lifelong learning in Ireland must be on those in the labour market.

Lifelong learning is generally regarded as having two aspects. One aspect is lifelong, the idea that people leave and re-enter education after having left the statutory system. The second aspect is life-wide and represents the view that learning takes place in a variety of situations and settings. Work-based learning is an example of lifewide learning. Only recently have we begun to value its outputs and systemise the accreditation of its results in such a way as to make them compatible with mainstream certification. Work-based learning must be to the fore in any future debate on lifelong learning.

The Information Age

We are living in an age which is characterised by the immediate availability of vast quantities of information over the Internet. We should bear in mind, however, that this is the latest development of the process which began with the printing press. Mass learning is a function of the cheap availability of the printed word. The ancient and medieval world saw learning as the function of priestly castes or orders. The revolution brought about by the printing press put an end to that.

By the nineteenth century, a system of free universal national schooling was in place throughout Northern Europe. This system was necessary to service the increasingly complex industrial society produced by the industrial revolution. New and more complex machinery spawned books of instructions and operating rules, which required a literate workforce to use them.

We are now coming to the end of the "command and control" industrial system which was a product of the industrial revolution. New forms of work organisation place greater emphasis on autonomy, and greater responsibility for on-the-job decisions. The concept of lifelong learning is an attempt by society to adapt the education and training system to this change.

Challenges to the Third-Level Sector

Writing in 1996, an OECD expert on lifelong learning stated that the universities had "missed the opportunity to organise their work so as to open their doors to a new clientele". This is a harsh judgement, but one applied to countries where up to 15–20 per cent of university entrants are classified as mature students. How much harsher this must seem in the Irish context where little over 5 per cent of full time university entrants are mature students.

Given the extent to which the demand for places has exceeded supply, younger people have tended to crowd out mature applicants. There are welcome signs that the universities are beginning to come to terms with this issue. Their commitment will ultimately be measured by their reaction to the proposals for mature entry quotas.

The greatest restriction on mature students, however, is finance, and this is beyond the control of the universities. If we are serious about lifelong learning, we must recognise the contradiction inherent in the position where mature entrants to third level who are not full-time undergraduates are charged tuition fees unless they are unemployed. This policy anomaly must be rectified if we are to continue to develop towards a high skills economy. The "universal versus means testing" debate for university education has been concluded inasmuch as a decision has been taken to pay fees for school leavers on a virtually universal basis. A priority for Congress in the near future will be the extension of that principle to mature students in employment.

Conclusion

Lifelong learning in Ireland is still at a formative stage. The recent Government Green Paper on Adult Education gives us a timely opportunity to advance the concept and to develop a workable model of lifelong learning that will suit Irish circumstances. The main emphasis of any system which emerges should be directed towards adults. The possibility of developing a new "educational guarantee" for each adult who has not completed the secondary system should be seriously debated between Government, employers, unions and providers.

At the beginning of the debate on lifelong learning, the emphasis was on equity, and on the need to facilitate people's full participation in society. In the 1980s, the emphasis shifted to a social aspect, with lifelong learning being seen as a means of combating mass unemployment. We are now moving to a time when the debate has assumed an economic aspect, with lifelong learning being assigned a key role in developing and upgrading the skills of those already in the labour force. All these three approaches have validity. Taken together, they will ensure that lifelong learning remains a key issue for Europe as we enter the new millennium.

References

European Centre for the Development of Vocational Training (1996), "Vocational Training", CEDEFOP: Thessaloniki, Greece.

OECD (1998), "Lifelong Learning — An Indicator Framework", November, OECD: Paris.

17

"Still Alien There?": Northern Protestants and the Irish Language Revival

Proinsias Ó Drisceoil

As has been pointed out by Garret Fitzgerald and others, proposals for increased North–South co-operation as contained in the Good Friday agreement are likely to involve concessions by the South to the North which may involve a level of ideological and administrative changes which the institutions of the South will find extremely painful. Intrinsic to this process will be the attempt to understand the cultural formation of the other side(s), as part of informed cultural debate. An instance of this is the need to engage imaginatively with the issues thrown up for Northern Protestants by the attempted Irish language revival. Language issues are likely to be central to future North–South co-operation in the field of education with implications ranging from teacher qualification to educational ideologies. Implicit in this issue is the relationship to the revival of Southern Protestants — sharing a religious affiliation with the Northern majority and a political affiliation to the Southern State — the perception of whose relationship to the revival is heavily coloured by the assumption that the Protestantism of

Douglas Hyde implied a general Protestant affiliation to the revival.

On 28 January 1994 I listened to a morning programme on Raidió na Gaeltachta about a native Irish speaker from Connemara who had lived in the Midlands for many years and who was that day celebrating his hundredth birthday in a Tullamore hospital. The programme was extensive and interesting, so when I came home that evening and saw the same man on the television news in English, I watched the interview. This time, however, the report was on his career as a member of the Royal Irish Constabulary, a fact never mentioned on Rádio na Gaeltachta; the television news on the other hand never mentioned the fact that he was a native Irish speaker!

This incident illustrates as well as any the evasions and unspoken ideologies which characterise much discussion on the Irish language. This habit of equivocation in the South, as Dennis Kennedy shows in his book *The Widening Gulf*, was a constant source of glee to Unionist newspaper columnists during the Free State years and any discussion on Unionists and the Irish language must proceed from the acknowledgement that the attempted language revival was for the majority of Protestants, in Kennedy's phrase, "an absurd fantasy, a dead horse". This was put a good deal less decorously by Sammy Wilson when he described Irish as a "leprechaun language".

Proponents of the language revival have adopted a number of arguments to counteract these perceptions. Principal of these has been to transfer the entire argument back to enlightenment Belfast, with Bunting, *Bolg an tSoláir* and the Belfast Harp Festival as moral tales for the present. Much interesting research has resulted but the relevance of the period for an understanding of the present is, in my view, a limited one, given that it was a time when Protestant fear of absorption into a larger entity did not apply and before Belfast's political, social and, above all, industrial character took their post-Union forms. Indeed, the descendants of those cultured liberals who organised the 1792 Belfast Harp Festival and who have left the Linen Hall Library as their monument sought cultural security in Unionism in the nineteenth century and most certainly were not proto-Gaelic Leaguers.

If instances of Presbyterian and Methodist involvement with the Irish language are being sought, the Evangelical Revival provides a precedent — however opportunistic and compromised the episode may have been in certain respects — of the worlds of evangelical religion and Gaelic culture interacting on the basis of exigency; the use of Irish in the Evangelical Revival constitutes the principal attempt in the nineteenth century to spread literacy in Irish. As David Hempton and Myrtle Hill (1992) have put it:

> From the mid-1820s copies of Irish Bibles, New Testaments and numerous tracts poured from the printing presses in response to the demands of the various preaching and teaching agencies. Despite their contrary intentions, therefore, early nineteenth-century evangelicals must take credit for at least slowing down the decline of the native tongue. They thus played a part, however unwittingly, in the preservation of the cultural heritage of Gaelic Ireland. Their enquiries into the state of the Irish language, and their extensive studies of its grammar and dialects, stimulated a new interest in its fate.

The denominational fractures and divisions within Irish Protestantism have been widely ignored by language revivalists, and by many academics who, in common with Roman Catholics in Ireland generally, have seen Irish Protestantism as an undifferentiated monolith. As a consequence, Anglican figures such as William Bedell, Robert Boyle and the Rev. John Richardson are often offered as encouraging examples to Protestants generally and the identity dilemma of Southern Anglicans is presumed to apply to Irish Protestantism as a whole.

Douglas Hyde, in his 1892 lecture on "The Necessity for De-Anglicising Ireland", acknowledged the scepticism of Northern Protestants towards any project of Gaelicisation, though hardly in language which they were likely to find appealing:

> . . . the north-east of Ulster, where the Gaelic race was expelled and the land planted with aliens, whom our dear mother Erin, assimilative as she is, has hitherto found it difficult to absorb . . . (quoted in Ó Conaire, 1986).

The subsequent history of the Gaelic League, however, largely ignored the unassimilable north-easterners and the concern of Hyde and other Protestant members was with the dilemma of belonging of the Protestant middle and gentry classes in the south, where their numbers were lowest. Growing politicisation caused many Protestant members eventually to drift away, but perhaps even more telling is the number of Gaelic League Protestants who converted to Roman Catholicism: Aodh de Blacam, Roger Casement, Mac Giolla Bhríde (Lord Ashbourne) and the folksong collector, Mrs Costello, were among the more prominent (Ó Glaisne, 1991).

Indeed, it could be argued that Hyde's campaigns on education, particularly his campaign to have Irish made a compulsory subject for entry to the new National University, did real damage to the prospect of Protestant participation in the Free State, establishing as it did compulsory Irish as critical to examination success and public service employment. While the Trinity of Mahaffy was unlikely to be other than hostile, Hyde's failure to deal realistically with the prospects for the teaching of Irish outside the Catholic denominational system had consequences which persist and it is surely ironic that when, in the Free State, Church of Ireland bishops and headmasters objected to the emphasis on compulsory Irish, the standard reply was that Hyde, who had been a Protestant, had set this measure in train and that therefore they had no cause for complaint (Giltrap, 1990).

The most consistent attempt to articulate from within nationalism an understanding of the difficulties presented for Northern Protestants by the language revival was made by Ernest Blythe (1889–1975). As is well known, Blythe was born at Magheragall, Lisburn, Co. Antrim and became a prominent language revivalist, a deputy in the first Dáil, a minister in the First Free State government, a leader of the Fascist Blueshirt movement and, eventually, director of the Abbey Theatre where he made artistic concerns secondary to the promotion of Irish. Contrary to what Oliver McDonagh (1983) and others have stated, Blythe was not a Presbyterian but rather a member of the Church of Ireland and his father had been from time to time a member of the diocesan synod (de Blaghd, 1957).

Blythe attributed to Irish speaking servant girls who had worked in his home his initial interest in Irish but a more likely explanation may be the conflict with his father which comes across strongly in his three-volume autobiography; the "otherness" of the language may well have given form to this antipathy, as well as offering focus and purpose to the shiftlessness of his early life.

Blythe saw religion as the principal line of division in Ireland and attributed the antipathy towards Irish nationalism of Northern Protestants to the South's failure to take the language issue seriously:

> . . . bhíodar . . . na Protastúnaigh . . . i gcoinne féinriail a bheith ag Éirinn; agus bhíodar amhlaidh toisc go raibh curtha ina luí orthu ag Caithlicigh na hÉireann, leis an slí inar thréigeadar-sin an Ghaeilge agus traidisiún a sinsear, nach mar chuspóir náisiúnta a bhíothas ag iarraidh greim Shasana a bhogadh d'Éirinn ach ar mhaithe

leis an chreideamh Caitliceach agus dada eile (de
Blaghd, 1955).

(Protestants were opposed to Irish self-government because Catholics, through their betrayal of the Irish language and ancestral tradition, had made it seem as if
they were not attempting to free England's grip on Ireland as a national aim but as a benefit to the Catholic
religion.)

Dennis Kennedy (1988) quotes the *Whig* of 27 April 1933 as
offering a comparable analysis, if with a political rather than a
religious emphasis and with, of course, very different conclusions. The demand for the teaching of Irish it said:

is one of the by-products of an agitation which is not cultural but political, having for its ultimate object the sev-
erance of the Province from the United Kingdom, and its
absorption into the Free State.

Whether one agrees with Blythe or not, his emphasis on the for-
tunes of the language in the South as crucial to attitudes in the
North is sustainable. It is in the South that a language revival
policy has been implemented by the state and it is there that the
language organisations have had their headquarters and greatest influence. Chris McGimpsey put the point well when he addressed a seminar on Unionists and the Irish language in 1992:

There is no reason why unionism should feel uncomfort-
able with the language if those who currently speak it
make an effort to facilitate this sea change in our
thinking. It can come about, but the catalyst must come
from that community which has claimed it as its own for
so long (quoted in Mistéal, 1994).

The leading proponents of the language revival were given a
unique opportunity to demonstrate their good faith in this regard when they addressed the special session of the Forum for

Peace and Reconciliation devoted to the language issue and held in Dublin Castle on 15 May 1995. It has to be said that with the exception of Ultach Trust, which is not in any event a specifically nationalist organisation, the presentations combined a degree of indifference, evasion and condescension towards the varieties of Irish Protestantism which indicated a failure to go beyond rhetoric and bluster to achieve a considered analysis of the place of the Irish language in a divided society.

The underlying assumptions in the presentations from Comhdháil Náisiúnta na Gaeilge — the national co-ordinating body for Irish language organisations — and Bord na Gaeilge — the quango established to promote the language — were Southern and Roman Catholic. For the witnesses from these bodies, Protestantism was a monolith without differentiation of class, geography or denomination. Furthermore, it had experienced no historic evolution and the complexities of the contemporary were conveniently evaded by shifting the question of the relationship between Protestants and the language back to sanitised and de-contextualised settings in the early days of the Gaelic League or even in the eighteenth century. At no point did the witnesses display a consciousness of the growing self-confidence and self-awareness of Ulster's regional culture nor was its distinctiveness recognised, let alone endorsed. Parity of esteem in law was sought for the Irish language but there was no reciprocal acknowledgement of the "otherness" of Ulster Protestant culture or its variety and richness.

Witnesses from these two bodies were clearly happier with transnational and EU-level aspects of the language issue and the UK government was urged to replicate its policies on Welsh and Scots Gaelic, without any reference to the wholly different circumstances created by the perception in Northern Ireland that one community has abrogated the language to itself, this in context of a war waged, in part, on the majority population (*Comhdháil Náisiúnta na Gaeilge* (1995)).

If these two submissions were characterised by evasion, no such accusation could be made against Conradh na Gaeilge, the oldest and largest of the voluntary language organisations. Conradh insisted that any arrangement for what it ambiguously called "Éire Nua" would give the Irish language a place at least equivalent to the place it enjoys in the 1937 Constitution, i.e. as the first national language, with English as a recognised second language. Irish, it said, should be taught in every school and a number of interim measures to cover the period to the attainment of this objective was tabulated. This does not, however, appear to have satisfied the organisation's membership which insisted in a motion, passed at an Ard-Fheis held on the same weekend, that Irish be a compulsory subject in every school in Ireland (Conradh na Gaeilge, 1995).

These policies could be characterised as cultural aggression directed at Northern Protestants at a time when attitudes to the language are beginning to thaw; alternatively, they could be interpreted as indicating a complete blindness to the world beyond nationalism. In either event, this is the politics of impossibilism. As it happens, the address by Chris McGimpsey to which I have referred dealt with the enforced teaching envisaged:

> In Northern Ireland it would be counterproductive to force Unionist children to learn Irish and would probably be viewed in a light similar to the black children in South Africa being forced to learn Afrikaans (Mistéal, 1994).

It might be noted in passing that Conradh na Gaeilge receives an annual grant of £176,000 from the Department of Arts, Culture and the Gaeltacht.

The submission from the Ultach Trust, which is the last with which I propose to deal, began by referring to the suspicion with which many Unionists view the Irish language. It went on to say that the language:

survived in Northern Ireland without the usual structures which enable minority languages to survive. There
was no State support. In fact the Irish language in
Northern Ireland faced enormous hostility from the
State until very recently. The language still had no official status. . . . Irish in Northern Ireland had no rooted
linguistic community. Its maintenance was entirely
based on the ideals of the revival.

It went on to say that:

out of the identity crisis now affecting Unionism, a
growing number of Unionists are themselves beginning
to redefine their identity in a way which can embrace
both an Irish cultural and a British political identity
(Ultach Trust, 1995).

The analysis offered by Ultach Trust seemed to owe something
to ideas on wholeness emanating from the Green ecological
movement. Thus, the Trust emphasised cultural continuity,
diversity and choice and the "validity of minority identities".
These insights, the Trust claims, have already become evident
in the South and offer Unionists a way into the language which
is non-threatening and, echoing McGimpsey, it placed a particular emphasis on those currently speaking Irish being prepared to create the accommodations necessary if curiosity is to
become participation.

It might be interesting to conclude this survey of issues sur-
rounding the relationship of Northern Protestants to the Irish
language with some empirical evidence on the extent to which
the teaching of Irish has succeeded among Protestants in the
South by cross-referencing the 1991 census returns on religious
affiliation with those for linguistic ability.

A number of caveats should be entered. Firstly, the question
on the census form which queries ability in Irish leaves it to
the individual to determine their level of fluency. The choice

was between "Irish only", "Irish and English", "read but cannot speak Irish", and those without Irish were to leave the box blank. As well as the high degree of subjectivity entailed by this self-assessment, the form-filling was inevitably inaccurate in some cases and linguists seeking out the sole Irish speaking Methodist monoglot or the three Presbyterians who similarly described themselves would be well advised to find an alternative research topic. The full table is as follows:

Table 1: Census 1991 — Population Classified by Religion and Ability to Speak Irish

Religious Denomination	Irish Only	Irish and English	Read but Not Speak Irish	Not Stated	Total Population
Roman Catholic	2,677	1,040,309	348,693	1,691,440	3,083,119
Church of Ireland	21	13,503	7,815	64,967	86,306
of which:					
Protestant	2	593	425	5,156	6,176
Presbyterian	3	1,672	1,181	9,842	12,698
Methodist	1	670	503	3,720	4,894
Jewish	0	129	253	1,151	1,533
Baptist	0	192	83	831	1,106
Quaker	0	167	54	510	731
Lutheran	0	69	16	903	988
Other religions of which:					
Christian (unspec.)	28	4,353	1,782	9,395	15,558
Muslim (Islamic)	4	201	82	3,147	3,434
Lapsed Rom. Cath.	3	1,246	605	1,846	3,700
Jehovah's Witness	2	525	341	2,404	3,272
Buddhist	1	95	40	830	966
Hindu	0	81	22	810	913
Latter Day Saints	1	194	62	548	805
Agnostic	0	278	113	430	821
Evangelical	1	121	88	570	780
Bahai	1	111	32	274	418
Greek Orthodox	0	22	17	304	343
Atheist	0	110	31	178	319
Apostic/Pentecostal	0	47	28	196	271
Brethren	0	36	23	194	253
Pantheist	0	67	15	115	197

Other stated denominations	1	403	166	1,532	2,102
No religion	39	15,085	5,753	42,536	63,413
Not stated	163	13,198	3,970	60,735	78,066
Total	2,946	1,092,884	371,768	1,899,408	3,367,006

Table 2: Principal Percentages of Ability to Speak Irish

	Irish Only	Irish and English	Read Irish but Not Speak	Not Stated
Roman Catholic	.08%	33.74%	11.30%	54.86%
Church of Ireland	.02%	15.64%	9.05%	75.27%
Presbyterian	.02%	13.16%	9.30%	77.50%
Methodist	.02%	13.69%	10.27%	76.00%
Jewish	0.0%	8.41%	16.50%	75.08%
Atheists	0.0%	34.48%	9.71%	55.79%
No religion	.6%	23.78%	9.07%	67.07%
Not stated	.20%	16.90%	5.08%	77.79%
Total	.08%	32.45%	11.04%	56.41%

Thus while just under half of Roman Catholics in the Republic claim a competence in Irish, under a quarter of Protestants claim a similar ability, and this figure is consistent across the various denominations. Thus the language revival in the South has had only modest success in breaking out of its point of relative strength in the Roman Catholic population.

On the basis of the submissions made to the Forum, one can hardly be persuaded that the language organisations based in the South are seriously attempting to break out of the corral.

None of this should be taken as implying that Irish speakers as a body are necessarily implicated in the statements of organisations to which, by and large, they have no particular affiliation. However, it remains the case that for the Irish language organisations based in the South, the varieties of Irish Protestantism are, to paraphrase John Hewitt, "still alien there" and an accommodation between Ulster Protestants and Gaelic revivalists is a distant prospect. Cultural assertion rather than cultural accommodation still dominates the field from every angle. If the building of informed self-confidence is to be a primary educational aim for this generation then the deconstruction of the ideologies which leave cultural formations blind to their own divisiveness is a necessary, indeed an urgent, political and educational task.

References

Aighneacht Chonradh na Gaeilge don Fhóram um Shíochán agus Athmhuintearas (1995).

Comhdháil Náisiúnta na Gaeilge (1995) An Ghaeilge sa Todhchaí: Fóram um Shíochán agus Athmhuintearas Bord na Gaeilge: An Fóram um Shíochain agus Athmhuintearas — Aitheasc Chathaoirleach Bhord na Gaeilge.

Conradh na Gaeilge (1995), Clár na hArd-Fheise, Trá Lí (rún a hocht)

de Blaghd, Earnán (1955), *Briseadh na Teorann*, Dublin.

de Blaghd, Earnán (1957), *Trasna na Bóinne*, Dublin.

Giltrap, Risteard (1990), *An Ghaeilge in Eaglais na hÉireann*, Dublin.

Hempton, David and Myrtle Hill (1992), *Evangelical Protestantism in Ulster Society 1740–1890*, London.

Kennedy, Dennis (1988), *The Widening Gulf, Northern Attitudes to the Independent Irish State 1919–49*, Belfast.

McDonagh, Oliver (1983), *States of Mind, A Study of Anglo-Irish Conflict, 1780–1980*, London.

Mistéal, Pilib (ed.) (1994), *The Irish Language and the Unionist Tradition*, Belfast.

Ó Conaire, Breandan, (ed.) (1986), "The Necessity for De-Anglicising Ireland" in *Language, Lore and Lyrics*, Dublin.

Ó Glaisne, Risteard (1991), *Dubhglas de hÍde, Ceannródaí Cultúrtha, 1860–1910*, Dublin.

Ultach Trust (1995), *The Irish Language in Northern Ireland*, submission to the Forum for Peace and Reconciliation, Dublin.

18

Coming of Age: Issues for the Institutes of Technology

Ed Riordan

The Institutes of Technology are often described as the most startling success story of modern Irish education, and it is not difficult to see why. From small beginnings in the 1960s, they now enroll more first year third-level students than their university counterparts. In every one of the Institutes, growth in student numbers has been quite extraordinary. For example, the chart below for total full-time students in Cork Institute of Technology indicates a pattern which is repeated around the country.

CIT Full-Time Third Level Students

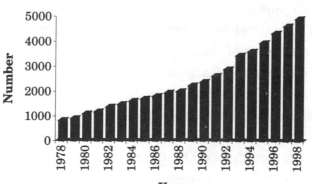

This explosion in student numbers took technological sector enrolments from 1,000 in 1965 to 35,000 in 1995. Another telling indicator of the growth of the Institutes is that, in most cases, they have already outstripped the projections for 2006/2007 set by the Steering Committee for the Future Development of Higher Education in 1995.

Not only have the older Institutes grown, the sector has been augmented by dynamic newcomers in Tallaght, Blanchardstown, Dun Laoghaire, Tipperary and Castlebar. Every year brings further expressions of confidence (and investment) in the sector from business, industry and government.

In observing this very impressive growth, there are a number of points which are worth noting. First, higher technological education did not commence in Ireland in the 1960s, rather it was much earlier; the rapid and sustained growth of the technological sector was based on a small but sound platform. The Royal Dublin Society, the Royal Cork Institution and the Belfast Academical Institution were active in promoting scientific and technological education in the early 19th Century, as somewhat later did similar Institutions in Galway and Limerick. The Mechanics Institutes, which flourished in every large town of Ireland in the mid-19th Century, gave instruction in all branches of mathematics, surveying, navigation, book-keeping and French among other subjects. However, they declined when the industrial base shrank before the end of the 19th Century, and most of them lived on in name but not in function. The setting up of a government Department of Agriculture and Technical Instruction in Dublin in 1900 was followed by a developed structure of local Technical Instruction Committees in most counties. The Vocational Education Act of 1930 set up a local and democratic framework. Some VECs, as well as running vocational schools, also managed third level colleges such as the Dublin Colleges of Technology and the Crawford Municipal Technical College in Cork. (A full account of these developments is to be found in *Teachers' Union — the History of the TUI* (1999), particularly the contribution by Professor Kieran Byrne.)

Suffice it to say that the occasionally-heard opinion that the Institutes of Technology were somehow an invention of the OECD and the World Bank is wide of the mark. Those agencies played their part, along with the Department of Education and many far-sighted policy makers and ministers. However, the Regional Technical Colleges were built on a solid foundation of technical educational tradition, and drew on the organisational base of the VECs. Most of all, their lecturing staff were continuing an identifiable and honourable tradition in Irish education. The competence and flexibility of those working in the technological sector in the 1969 to 1974 period, when the RTCs opened, gave their institutions a flying start.

A second point regarding the spectacular growth of the sector is that this has not been a smooth passage — there have been (and still are) difficulties of execution and strongly divergent opinions about the role and standing of the Institutes.

The Department of Education and its advisors have had a dread of academic drift; that the colleges would chase degree awards to the detriment of certificate, diploma and apprenticeship courses. In the early years, some thought that the idea of a degree qualification in a Regional Technical College was outlandish. The government in 1975 proposed strict limits on degrees and that they would be validated by universities. This policy was reversed in 1978. The Department of Education policy was that two-year technician certificates were the core business of the sector.

The colleges and the NCEA have opted for academic stretch rather than academic drift. They have built on to certificate courses a ladder of progression via diploma to degree awards.

(There are, of course, many ab-initio degree courses too.) The flexibility for the student and for the employer offered by this arrangement is very attractive — especially when coupled to part-time, evening or credit-accumulation (ACCS) study. For example, a student with a certificate who takes up employment can subsequently add diploma and degree levels over a period of years, often with company support. It is also significant that CAO points levels for entry to this "ladder" are not excessive, while the ultimate award can be an honours degree or post-graduate qualification.

Even with strong demand for degree level technology graduates and the flexibility offered by the ladder system, it is fair to say that for most of their history the Institutes of Technology have had an uphill struggle to get approval for their degree work. As recently as 1995, the Steering Committee on the Future Development of Higher Education recommended that, across the sector in the short-term, degree output should be kept under 20% of those graduating. For good measure, seven tests were proposed before approval would be given for new degree programmes.

While separately some of the criteria looked reasonable, (proven demand for the course; course geared to needs of industry, etc.) the overall impression given to many Institute of Technology academics was negative and patronising.

In fairness to those who expressed fears about academic drift if the Institutes leaned too heavily towards degree provision, it must be admitted that there are many precedents abroad and some at home for such drift. The pressure is strong — not least from parents and prospective students who think of higher education only in terms of "getting a college degree".

The steady growth of add-on degrees in the technological sector can be readily justified, however. They offer:

- Greater flexibility for the student

- A wider range of specialised graduates available to industry

- A route to higher qualifications and career development for those already at work

- The ladder of progression is the only current working system for easing the points race

- Technological degree level graduates are the "feedstock" for research and development in industry and in the Institutes.

Over the past few years, the argument for artificial numerical capping of degree graduates from Institutes of Technology has become plain silly. The Institutes' capacity to deliver quality graduates with relevant and sought after qualifications has put the issue to bed.

The Institutes of Technology, particularly the Dublin Institute of Technology (DIT) and Cork Institute of Technology (CIT), have had a long association with craft training across a huge spectrum of trades. All the colleges once had a significant apprentice education role. In the eighties, the economic downturn and a policy of centralisation of provision by the Department of Education led to the virtual extinction of apprentice classes in a majority of the colleges, the principal remaining centres being Cork, Dublin, Galway, Sligo and Limerick. While this decline was vigorously opposed by the staff involved and by the Teachers' Union of Ireland, it may not have been viewed as a calamity by some college directors anxious to develop more prestigious courses.

A further problem for apprentice education appeared in 1990 when FÁS proposed a "new apprenticeship" scheme which, as initially planned, would have drastically reduced the education content of training. A two-year training period was proposed to replace the existing four-year apprenticeship. Again, a vigorous campaign ensued which gained the support of college staffs, the Department of Education and many concerned industry groups. The final shape of the scheme preserved the essential educational elements. This, coupled with the strong economic upturn of the mid-nineties, has rewarded those Institutes which kept faith with apprenticeship with greater than ever demand — now followed by multi-million pound State investment.

The Institute of Technology sector has been quite clear that one of its main objectives is to meet the needs of industry and business. This is evident for example in the Regional Technical Colleges Act, 1992, and a scan of the mission statements of each college confirms how high this aspect rates in their priorities. This is as it should be; after all, it was the glaring lack of higher education and training to meet the economic growth of the sixties that brought the RTCs into being. So how have the colleges attempted to meet this goal?

- First, the graduates from certificate, diploma and degree courses are the bearers of a highly relevant qualification. Programmes generally include high proportions of laboratory and project work along with the appropriate theory.

- The enormous changes in the economy have been mirrored by the development and expansion of new courses in the Institutes. Not only has this catered for the education and training needs of mainstay industries such as electronics and the chemical industry, but whole new industry sectors such as biotechnology and software development have spawned courses in the Institutes. The existence of these courses has, in turn, been a powerful magnet for further investment.

- There has been a strong element of staff recruitment from industry into lecturing posts in the colleges, which has an obvious benefit in ensuring the relevance of courses and structures. A recent agreement, negotiated under the PCW, which appears to limit recruitment to a relatively low-paid Assistant Lecturer grade may have a negative impact on the healthy pattern of industry–college transfer. If that transpires, it will be detrimental to the future not just of the colleges but also of the economy. For the present, the Institutes of Technology have on their staffs a very considerable number of lecturers with industrial experience.

• Another guarantee of the relevance of courses is the input from industry-based external examiners and course assessors who review the work of the colleges. About one-fifth of all external reviewers are from industry.

• As well as providing graduates with industry-relevant qualifications, the colleges offer routes to upgrade qualifications for those in the workplace. Part-time evening study and the (ACCS) credit accumulation scheme are used to step up the "ladder". Many companies support individuals and whole groups in such further professional education. Indeed, colleges sometimes design specific courses to meet the requirements of particular employers or industry groups.

• Research and development activity in the Institutes is growing rapidly. This work covers the full spectrum from pure basic research for the advancement of knowledge, through applied research to product and process development. It is fair to say that most research in the Institutes is in the applied category. This applied research effort is often based in Centres of Expertise which offer consultancy, applied research and product development services to industry. Examples in Cork Institute of Technology are the Clean Technology Centre and the Biological and Environmental Services Unit.

A problem which inhibits research, consultancy and development work is that the basic lecturing workload in the Institutes is higher than in the universities. This is not stated as a criticism of either sector. However, it seems obvious that if a lecturer has the ideas, ambition and projects for more research, then the Institute system must develop more flexibility to allow this work to be done.

What we have, therefore, is a picture of a sector which has grown in scale, variety and sophistication. It is a sector which can trace its formal origins in the main cities to the early 19th century, and which was given the job of meeting the needs of the open and growing economy which came into being in the mid-1960s.

Those working within the Institutes of Technology will know that, apart from grand policy matters, the task of coping with such a major increase in student numbers has been very demanding. Lecturers have been faced with larger and larger groups, often in lecture rooms which are crowded, unsuitable and uninspiring — a legacy of the original "Legoland" style of RTC architecture. Management and administrators have faced enormous problems with inadequate staff numbers, while student services and facilities are only now beginning to get a fair level of funding. Such problems are not unique to the technological sector or indeed to Ireland, but it is important to remember that the success of the enterprise has not been won without pain.

On a policy and resources level, the Institutes of Technology are better placed than ever. Successive governments and Ministers have placed heavy demands in terms of student intake on the colleges, and have been impressed with the response. The current Minister, Mícheál Martin, has been outspoken in expressing confidence in the sector, a confidence matched by him with significant investment.

All of which brings us, in a roundabout way, to the binary system. Stated public policy is that within higher education we have two main strands, the technological sector and the university sector. While there are no absolutely clear dividing lines, the Institutes generally are comfortable with a binary classification that sees them as:

- Partners of equal standing with the universities

- Having a specific focus of directly serving the needs of the economy

- Offering flexible programmes at a variety of levels - craft, certificate, diploma, degree and postgraduate

- Developing research activity which, while not being artificially limited, is of an oriented and applied nature.

On the "other side" of the binary divide are the universities, including the NUI universities, Trinity College, University of Limerick and Dublin City University. Their programmes cover a wider spectrum of disciplines than do the Institutes', and basic research is encouraged. They do not offer a ladder of progression to degree level, and do not have as explicit a goal of industrial relevance as the Institutes of Technology.

Of course the binary system is not the only workable model for higher education, but with a few bruises and scrapes it survives and prospers today in Ireland. Two institutions (NIHE Limerick and NIHE Dublin) have transferred from the technological sector and have respectively become University of Limerick and Dublin City University. They are both outstanding institutions with distinct "personalities". The question arises therefore as to whether, in the fullness of time, some or indeed all of the Institutes of Technology might follow the same path. That would appear to involve the break-up of the current binary model, and some might argue "so what, if the country ended up with a network of fine universities?".

Several events of recent years have raised the temperature of the debate. Minister of the day Niamh Bhreathnach announced an intended upgrading and re-titling of Waterford RTC to Waterford Institute of Technology in January 1997. The reaction of Cork RTC, which had been campaigning for the title of Cork Institute of Technology, was immediate, public and furious, and was echoed in the other RTCs to a lesser extent. While Waterford argued for special consideration on grounds of under-provision of degree places in the South East, it became clear that Cork and some others would not permit such a similar institution to gain a higher designation, powers and probably funding. Minister Bhreathnach conceded a review process to Cork and Waterford to consider devolving to both colleges the power to make their own awards. She proposed that such reviews would be the key to Institute of Technology status for colleges other than Waterford, on which she had already bestowed the title. This new policy was logical, but was soon overtaken by events.

With the change of government in June 1997, Mícheál Martin became Minister and in October 1997 he announced his intention to re-title Cork RTC as Cork Institute of Technology. This was followed by a similar change of title for all the former RTCs in February 1998.

In October 1998, the Review Group led by Professor Dervilla Donnelly recommended that Cork Institute of Technology and Waterford Institute of Technology should be given authority to make awards up to diploma level. With the vexed question of title resolved, those two institutions are currently preparing to implement their greater academic autonomy, the final shape of which is being decided by the National Qualifications Bill, 1999, now enacted.

Meanwhile, Dublin Institute of Technology pressed a claim for university status — not without misgivings from some staff and students — using Section 9 of the Universities Act, 1997.

The report of DIT's Review Group set out several areas for development, but was favourable to the idea of university status in three to five years. Initial euphoria in DIT evaporated when the Higher Education Authority and the Minister decided that a further full Section 9 review process would be needed when and if DIT reapplied for university status. In effect, a post-dated cheque for DIT's university status was politely but firmly cancelled. It appears that state policy is unenthusiastic about attempts to pole-vault across the binary divide.

So let us assume that the binary system, including DIT, will remain intact in its broad outlines for the foreseeable future. What challenges does the technological sector face?

Total enrolments will continue to rise, driven by several factors. These include an upward trend in the participation rate in higher education among the school-leaving cohort; strong growth in mature student numbers, from a base which is far below European and OECD norms; improved perception of the standing of the Institutes of Technology; and likely continued investment in them to meet skills needs of the economy.

The proportion of degree-level graduates will increase. This will involve some tensions as the Institutes and the Department of Education grapple with the question of academic stretch versus academic drift. Nevertheless, the Institutes will aim to offer a path to a degree qualification for every entrant.

The Institutes of Technology will have to be far more structured and pro-active in their attempts to promote equality of opportunity. Higher education is a highly subsidised engine of social inequality. Differences in participation rates among the various socio-economic groups are so great as to be a national scandal. It is true that participation rates in the technological sector from the manual worker categories are roughly twice those for the universities (1992 figures). This is cold comfort; participation from the three highest socio-economic categories is around ten times greater.

The learning environment of the Institutes is in the process of being transformed. The grey concrete sprawl of the original RTCs may have been functional, but those rectilinear block-houses were unlovely and unloved. New libraries, information technology centres, student centres and lecture halls of great architectural merit are replacing them. Likewise, student services such as careers advice, student counselling, medical and sports facilities are expanding. These improvements will go a long way to eliminating any public perception of the sector as being a poor relation of the universities.

For thirty years, the Institutes of Technology have been marking out a substantial territory in the higher education landscape. They have been hampered at times by official timidity, by inadequate resources and buildings, and by an inaccurate public perception of their worth. With their new titles and expanding academic powers these colleges are more intellectually self-confident than ever. If that self-confidence is matched by government funding and real parity of esteem, the Institutes of Technology will become not just an Irish but a world model for success.

19

Looking Back to Look Forward
The City of Dublin VEC and
Adult Education

Jim Cooke

The word "school" is derived from the Greek word *skholé* meaning leisure, the leisure to sit around the fountains of Athens or stroll through the groves of Academe disputing philosophy and law, or engaging in fine arts and sports. School was confined to the aristocratic and rich and it remained the preserve of these for many centuries, while the apprentice toiled away in the workshop, and the clerk in the counting-house.

In Ireland there was an ancient tradition of liberal-cum-vocational Brehon education, followed by the great tradition of monastic scholarship and fine art. It was not until the Industrial Revolution of the 1790s that the need for practical scientific education began, as a form of adult education.

The Dublin Mechanics' Institute was founded in 1824 and provided a system of lectures, demonstrations and library/reading-room facilities for the inquisitive workman to try to grasp the underlying scientific principles and processes of his trade. But it was not until the widespread provision of primary education following the setting up of the 1831 National Education system that the mechanics' institutes (of which there were 28 in Ireland) could have some real effect, with the addition of classes to their programme. By the 1840s the Dublin Mechanics' Institute held evening classes in geometry, French, architectural and mechanical drawing and, by 1842, classes in dancing, music, chemistry, mathematics, writing, arithmetic and English grammar. There were 50 students in the mathematical class covering algebra, geometry, bookkeeping, mensuration, writing and arithmetic; 25 students in the English grammar class; 14 students in French; 15 in the piano forte and vocal music class; 30 in the drawing class; and 25 in the chemistry class. The library was well stocked with a daily loan of 87 books.

In 1844 the *Freeman's Journal* commented that "a knowledge of the French language is considered equally essential to the man of business as to the scholar", which has a very modern ring to it.

When Dublin Corporation decided to set up its own evening technical school, following the Dublin Artisans' Exhibition of 1885, it negotiated with the Dublin Mechanics' Institute to take over its premises for that purpose. Although this proposal failed and a Kevin Street site was chosen in 1887, when the Dublin Mechanics' Institute was wound up in 1919 the proceeds of the liquidation were converted into a scholarship fund for the students of Bolton Street, and this is now part of a consolidated scholarship fund for the City of Dublin Vocational Education Committee.

The technical schools at Kevin Street were the first such schools in Ireland and conducted all their classes at night, after the students had finished their work. This was the pattern of all technical schools for many years. The subjects taught were closely related to the science, technology and commerce of the workplace and constituted the first and abiding category of adult education.

When the City of Dublin VEC (CDVEC) was established under the 1930 Vocational Education Act through the integration of the technical instruction schemes of the City of Dublin, the Pembroke Township and the Rathmines Township, while some day classes were in operation, the main body of students attended at night. The City of Dublin brought evening trade classes and art and design classes which enrolled 4,700 night students comprising about 12,000 individual class enrolments. The Rathmines school provided evening classes in commerce and domestic economy with an approximate enrolment of 1,620 representing about 4,804 class entries. Pembroke brought three evening trade courses, a commerce and languages course, a domestic economy course and a handicraft course, and enrolment figures were of the same order.

Following the 1930 Act there was a slow shift from night courses to day courses. From 1946 Kevin Street provided a correspondence course for ESB apprentices in the preparation stage for "rural electrification". This was a unique CDVEC use of a mode of adult education more noted in the vast spaces of Australia and New Zealand.

Together with the vocational, technical and professional evening courses provided by the CDVEC — e.g. Rathmines specialised in accountancy, legal and business studies, while Parnell Square specialised in the marketing and design areas — the education for "self-fulfilment", or learning for its own sake, was promoted in CDVEC schools. One example of this type of adult education was the pottery class in North Strand Vocational School. During the 1956 Hungarian Rising the Department of Foreign Affairs arranged for Hungarian refugees to be brought to Ireland and the CDVEC took on (with the aid of a German interpreter) Mr Laszio Lovas as a potter. He started the famous pottery classes in North Strand, continued as a legend under Bill O'Brien (now of Coolock). Also in the 1950s, Shelbourne Road school ran courses for brides-to-be, and also cookery classes for the blind in association with the League for the Blind of Ireland. A gardening guild met in

Cabra Vocational School while the CDVEC employed the services of a Department of Agriculture expert on horticulture and bee-keeping for its various out-schemes. Many lectures on civic, community, literary and public affairs were conducted in Rathmines Town Hall and other centres. The CDVEC was a hive of adult education activities. It justly prided itself on responding to every request for adult education services and also initiated many vocational, technical, commercial and professional courses at night, which subsequently would transfer to the status of whole time day courses, while continuing to provide for the needs of the less financially independent night students. The list of all these courses literally filled a good-sized book. The CDVEC has always been the largest individual provider of adult education in the country.

With the second coming of Vocational Education in the 1960s, following the *Investment in Education* report, an additional programme of adult education evolved in the CDVEC: one of remedial education, both literacy programmes and second-chance courses for Group Certificate and later for Leaving Certificate.

Following the founding of the adult education association, Aontas, in 1969, the first pilot adult literacy project in Ireland was started by a Catholic Dublin diocesan agency, the Dublin Institute of Adult Education, funded by a grant from the CDVEC. Since then a vast network of literacy, self-empowerment and community-empowerment classes and workshops have been created under the auspices of the CDVEC. Second chance mainstream education facilities are also provided and a large project of VTOS (Vocational Training Opportunities Scheme) has been introduced whereby unemployed adults can return to mainstream education of any variety to acquire education and vocational skills in the schools.

It has long been recognised that there is a higher demand for adult education where there is a growing proportion of young people going to higher or further education. This higher demand for adult education is also a feature of a country's higher economic activity where technical obsolescence creates the demand for vocational retraining. This is noticeable now in the world of computers, almost on a yearly basis. Where technology leads, catch-up education becomes a practical survival requirement in employment, trade and commerce. Where the young take to new technology like ducks to water, adults have to get themselves into the same adaptive mode of operations.

There are three official landmarks on the landscape of modern Irish adult education: the Con Murphy *Adult Education in Ireland* report of 1973; the Ivor Kenny *Lifelong Learning* report of 1984; and the current green paper "Adult Education in an Era of Lifelong Learning". The latter is dealt with by Kevin Hurley in Chapter 15 of this book.

The Murphy Report (1973) was the first modern attempt to survey the field of adult education and made very far-seeing recommendations which have gradually been implemented. Meanwhile, on the ground, the CDVEC and other organisations beavered away at an expanding provision of adult education. The first concrete result of the Murphy Report came with the appointment of Adult Education Officers to the VECs in 1979 — six for the City of Dublin — and ever since then they have been key figures in spreading adult education in the community while being anchored in the schools' ever-expanding provision.

The Kenny Report (1984) was immediately acted on by the Department of Education with the invocation of Section 21 of the 1930 Vocational Education Act to appoint Adult Education Boards in each VEC area. The functions of these boards were to assess the adult education needs within each area; prepare an annual programme of activities and estimates of expenditure; administer the agreed programme, while reporting to both the Minister and the VEC; and undertake any further duties requested by the Minister. The comprehensive nature of powers and the statutory nature of the VEC's constitution ensures a lasting and structured system to expand the provision of adult education.

The new Green Paper "Adult Education in an Era of Lifelong Learning" (1998) presents the best opportunity to date to transform the old moulds of school and factory, home and office, into ones of power — of self-empowerment and creative insight and energy.

When black curtains were drawn across the windows of the Municipal School of Music with the outbreak of war in September 1939, the CDVEC decided that music (night) classes would go on as usual, despite danger, shortage of supplies, and transport difficulties, and music-making became a great symbol and source of joy and hope in those following bleak years. In a time of peace and seeming plenty, the fundamental needs of people must be met in a new way, and now is the time to affirm, and construct, a system of lifelong learning which will empower and enrich all our lives.

References

Byrne, Kieran R. (1976), "Mechanics' Institutes in Ireland before 1855" (Unpublished M.Ed. thesis, UCC).

City of Dublin VEC, Minutes, 1930 ff.

Cooke, James J. (1982), "The Movement for a Separate Department for Technical Instruction in Ireland, with Particular Reference to the Role of Dublin Corporation, 1867-1902" (Unpublished M. Litt thesis, TCD).

20

Aspects of Irish Education and Training in a European Context

Richard Langford

During the 1990s Ireland has enjoyed some significant successes in economic growth and social progress, at least in relative international terms. GNP per capita has increased from under 75 per cent of the EU average and is now rapidly converging with the average. Our demographic profile is markedly different from most of EU partners, giving rise to reducing dependency ratios while those of most member states are moving in the other direction. The high level of net new jobs created each year, with net employment creation in the last four years exceeding the aggregate of the previous thirty years, has meant that unemployment levels have dropped from the inordinately high percentages of the mid 1980s/early 1990s to below the EU average and are still falling — this despite the major net increase in the size of the labour force itself.

The factors which underlie Ireland's recent successes are many and complex. However, all commentators are agreed that the crucial variables include key decisions taken in relation to education and training more than thirty years ago and the continued investment in human capital development which has followed. These decisions have meant that the overall structure of the Irish education system, and particularly our approach to vocational education and training, differ significantly from the structures and approaches to be found in many other European countries.

There is no single global approach to the organisation of education and training systems which has been applied in all countries. There are, however, similarities of approach between many countries. In an address to a 1994 Congress in Hannover organised by the German Federal Ministry of Education and Science and the German Federal Institute of Vocational Training (BIBB), David Soskice identified two very broad and very different models of education and training provision:

- The Northern European Model as evidenced particularly in Germany, Austria, Switzerland and the Netherlands

- The Anglo-Saxon model, possibly more appropriately titled Anglo-American, which has operated especially in the UK, USA, Canada, Australia and New Zealand and which is also reflected in the Irish experience.

The most distinctive feature of these two models is that a large proportion of young people in the North European model have traditionally opted for serious vocational training on completion of the compulsory education phase at age 15/16. Their counterparts in the Anglo-American model have been more likely to continue in a form of general education at that stage, with vocational or occupational specific development being deferred to the post-secondary education stage at age 18 and then very often being provided within higher and further education institutions rather than in dedicated vocational training centres.

The North European Model in the area of vocational education and training has existed for over a century, founded on a high degree of social partnership and consensus. Very active involvement by business and industry is facilitated in certain countries, for example, in Germany by the public law status of the Industrie and Handelskammer and the Handwerskammer. This gives a key role to the workplace in determining the content of the learning as well as mode and place of its provision (generally alternance-based) and in certifying the outcomes. On the other hand the Anglo-American model most prevalent in Ireland with its extended general education provision probably gives a stronger basis on which to build a lifelong learning model. Also, because it is not as constrained by the requirements of a multiplicity of specific occupations, it is often more flexible and adaptable and does not appear to give rise to overlong lead times in bringing about change. In addition, while the wish for parity of esteem is a feature of both systems, it seems to pose a more fundamental difficulty in the North European model.

The changes in the workplace as we move increasingly to an information-based and service-dominated society have given rise to corresponding changes in identifying and providing for the skills and qualification requirements of that society. While the two broad models of education and training systems, to which I have referred earlier, may be based on different assumptions, the challenges posed for them by our developing society are leading to their convergence in many respects. The employer-led North European system, with its emphasis on specific occupations, is increasingly cognisant of the need to give a central place to the development of core skills and competences as a basis for lifelong learning, and to facilitate the greater level of job mobility which will be the norm for employees in the future.

Equally, many of those involved in Anglo-American models seem to acknowledge the need for a far more direct and positive involvement than has been the practice heretofore of workplace interests in curriculum development and in the provision, accreditation and certification of learning.

With regard to the future, the increasing significance of lifelong learning will require great diversity of provision in relation to the time, mode and place. There is a need to move from the tyranny of the current preoccupation with "whole" qualifications to a recognition of the value of learning. The education system has traditionally provided programmes leading to "whole awards" that are very age-specific and time-based. Many accreditation processes start with identifying the requirements for a whole qualification or a whole programme, with credits awarded for parts of programmes — as a deconstruction of the whole, and having value only in that context — as sub-sets of something larger.

Stakeholders' interests will be best served by credit-based approaches which provide recognition of learning achievement, in small chunks, as worthy of an award in its own right. The requirements for a specific qualification can then be identified in terms of a range of credits (number, level and/or type) that satisfy the requirements for that award. Learners may choose to accumulate credits towards a defined qualification - or indeed choose not to as they see fit. Credits gained must be transferable to other institutions, awards and pathways, if they are appropriate to that context. Employers also need a means of understanding the nature of the achievement of potential employees, and need to gain appropriate recognition for the learning opportunities they provide in the workplace, and elsewhere, for their employees.

In Ireland, we have given much consideration recently to the possible establishment of a single national qualifications framework for all post-second level education and training, other than in the seven universities. It is in that context that I came into contact, and worked closely, with Michael Enright through our membership of TEASTAS — the interim Irish National Certification Authority charged with advising on the legislative underpinning for the development of such a framework.

TEASTAS advised that this legislation should provide for a single National Qualifications Authority with strong linkages both to the seven universities and to the general education system at second level. Also, that this Authority should include representation from all relevant stakeholders and have responsibility, inter alia, for:

- Approving and auditing implementation of the quality assurance procedures of the awarding bodies within the framework

- Establishing and maintaining a credit framework

- Guaranteeing satisfactory transfer and progression mechanisms for the holders of qualifications from the awarding bodies and facilitating similar progression arrangements with the university system

- Mutual recognition arrangements with parallel frameworks in other countries to facilitate transnational progression and mobility of learners and workers.

TEASTAS was of the view that the primary focus, in moving forward towards the development of this national qualifications framework, must be the requirements of the individual learners. Whatever qualifications system is developed, accessibility and understanding for the learner is the key issue. This preoccupation with ensuring that the learner's needs are central, and particulary that access, progression, transfer and mobility must be prerequisites of any future arrangements, was an abiding concern of Michael Enright in his many considered contributions to the TEASTAS deliberations.

Obviously, it is essential also that the quality of all awards within the framework is certain. Mechanisms are needed to ensure that the certifying bodies are confident that awards are being made only where satisfactory standards have been attained. The issue arises here of what needs to be done both practically and in legislation to achieve this. In my view it is not enough to merely measure attainments/competences at the end of the process. Certification also has to be about putting in place mechanisms to ensure that the outputs will all be of a satisfactory standard and to oversee and monitor both the outputs and the quality assurance mechanisms of programme providers and awarding bodies.

While the work of TEASTAS commenced under the aegis of Niamh Bhreathnach, Minister for Education in the previous Government, it has continued without interruption under the current administration. This reflects the broad political support which exists for the putting in place of a revised system of qualifications and awards, which is aimed not just at tidying up and streamlining the previous plethora of arrangements for the making of awards, but which is designed to accredit learning in all its forms in a lifelong learning society. The Qualifications (Education and Training) Bill (1999) introduced in the Oireachtas by the present Minister for Education and Science, Mícheál Martin and since enacted, draws extensively on the advice of TEASTAS. It provides for the establishment of an overarching National Qualifications Authority, for two major Awards Councils — for higher education and training and further education and training respectively — and for the inclusion within the overall framework of the qualifications and awards processes of the Dublin Institute of Technology. It also contains creative proposals for ongoing linkages with the universities and with the National Council for Curriculum and Assessment, and provides significant safeguards for the financial as well as the academic interests of learners. Michael Enright's contribution to the development of this legislation has been valuable and I have no doubt its enactment and implementation will reflect his interest and concern for the needs of all learners and other stakeholders.

21

Towards the Learning Society: Responsiveness and Accountability

Micheál Martin

Context

Worldwide strategies for coping with change are giving effect to new and vastly different ways of living and working. Yet we are only at the beginning of these change patterns as we now stand on the verge of previously unimagined developments in information and communications technology. These extraordinary events are placing new tools and extremely powerful resources and capabilities at the disposal of all our citizens, and are driving revolutionary change much more emphatically towards the realisation of the world as a virtual global village.

The effects of change on the way we live and work are particularly striking. We are fast approaching the point where living and working are, together, becoming synonymous with learning. A 1997 publication, for example, by the Secretary's Commission on Achieving Necessary Skills in the United States emphasises this point in its title – *Learning a Living: A Blueprint for High Performance in the Workplace*. Formal learning in education and training institutions is being supplemented and replaced by learning at work, in the home, in the community and in recreational settings.

There is little doubt that social, cultural and economic life is increasingly dependent on our capacity to learn continuously and rapidly. The tools to support these developments are fast becoming available to people in general as miniaturisation continues to advance, costs continue to fall and vast stores of new knowledge enter our living rooms instantly through the medium of world-wide electronic networks. The World Wide Web, now only in its infancy, is about to grow to adult proportions virtually overnight in the full multimedia glory of text, voice, sound and pictures. In short, we are only a small step away from having a global university in our own homes.

Against this background, we cannot fail to consider the possibilities of mass education, never previously an issue but now essential, on an enormous basis of diversity and individual choice. Clearly, in what is becoming known as the massification of education, the entire gamut of ways of learning must be exploited for the optimum benefit of all. This has major implications for our education and training institutions, for the workplace, and for the way we live and function in our homes and communities.

Placing the Focus on Learners and Learning

In considering the relevant issues, the first fundamental criterion is that students or, more generally, learners of whatever hue, must be placed at the centre of all policies, strategies and systems of learning. Decisions on how we respond to the changing world in which we now live inevitably hinge on the changing learning needs and requirements of our people. Obviously, on this account also, the traditional primacy of institutions, agencies and communities must be open to necessary change and development. The centrality of learners in the provision of education and training has been a core criterion of the Government's educational policy since coming to office in mid-

1997 and is essential to developing the characteristics of lifelong learning.

As far back as 1976, the General Council of UNESCO
adopted a definition of lifelong learning which placed the
learner firmly at the centre:

> The term "lifelong education and learning" denotes an
> overall scheme aimed both at restructuring the existing
> education system and at developing the entire educa-
> tional potential outside the education system; in such a
> scheme, men and women are the agents of their own
> education.

Lifelong learning therefore involves the achievement of a
learning society — a paradigm in which more active learning
at all levels becomes systemic to and part of the life ethic of a
particular society or population.

Building the Learning Society

The lifelong learning culture underpinning the learning society
must be flexible, creative and responsive. It will require teachers to function more as facilitators and consultants. Such a culture is characterised by a range of imperatives which dictate
that education must serve the needs of people rather than the
reverse, so that:

- Both individualised and collective learning can be based on
  negotiation between teachers and learners.

- Provision is flexible allowing the content of learning to be
  assimilated at such times and in such situations as to suit
  the learners.

- The absence of prescription enables learners to progress at
  a pace and in a direction that meets their individual needs.

- The elimination of unnecessary distinctions between different institutions and learning workplaces helps to streamline and unify credit arrangements.

- Authority over the learning process can be realised by relevant individual, organisation and community interests.

In building the learning society, in a world wide context, it is essential that we take cognisance of our own national position in the first instance and in particular our membership of the European Union. Secondary to that is the pressing need to consider the diversity of issues relating to the information and communications technology revolution not only from the Irish and European Union standpoints but also in communication with other areas and continents throughout the world.

The work of international agencies such as UNESCO, the OECD, the European Parliament and the Nordic Council of Ministers has focused on a variety of themes having broad implications for the developing learning society, such as:

- Increasing awareness of the importance of the concepts of the knowledge economy and the learning society.

- Growing acceptance of the need for a new philosophy of education and training in which institutions of all kinds have new roles and responsibilities for learning — formal and informal, public and private, traditional and alternative.

- Ensuring that the foundations for lifelong learning are achieved by all citizens during the years of compulsory education.

- Promoting articulation between schools, workplaces, further and higher education centres, and other agencies offering opportunities for learning over the individual lifespan.

- Providing opportunities for stakeholders, including the social partners, to invest in lifelong learning.

- Ensuring that emphasis on the learning society does not reinforce privilege or widen the gap between the advantaged and disadvantaged for access to education.

As I have stated earlier, the increasingly easy availability of vast quantities of information and knowledge is a major aspect to be taken into account in the future. A key role of future providers of education and training lies in achieving intelligent access to and effective use of this resource. The selection and development of methods and modes of learning will be key to the appropriate filtering and use of relevant knowledge from the vast networks of available information. It will be essential for teachers to be learners too, organising knowledge and using the results of research to provide a consultative resource for learners. In this way, learners will be able to engage more proactively in the learning process through the resources and supports provided by teachers, consultants, researchers and publishers.

The education system is set to become a proactive and responsive element of society, influencing and being influenced by the dynamics of that society. In doing so, it must function amidst the tensions of a quality circle. Those tensions include the need to be authoritative while embracing partnership and allowing for the achievement of the principle of subsidiarity. Authority demands accountability which does not always sit easily with traditional concepts of academic freedom and the spirit of education. Partnership on the other hand demands, *inter alia*, mutual respect, equality, co-operation, harmony and teamwork. Finally, subsidiarity requires not only decentralisation of action to the optimum extent but the free flow of information, knowledge and power in all directions throughout the societal network — including from the centre to the extremities.

A complex interdependent relationship has also been recognised between three specific processes of lifelong learning that are crucial to the learning society:

- Personal development leading to a more satisfying and rewarding lifestyle

- Education for a more highly skilled workforce

- Creating a stronger and more inclusive society.

At present, these processes are initiated and supported in the home, and continued and actualised through pre-school, primary, secondary, higher, further, workplace, adult and community education. The learning society presents new possibilities for blurring the distinctions and eliminating barriers between types and levels of educational provision, and for the realisation of a greater sense of the education continuum throughout life.

Milestones Towards the Learning Society

I am very pleased to have had the responsibility to date for instituting a range of initiatives which I believe will provide important milestones and landmarks towards the achievement of the learning society. The following is a selection of practical and key examples which are the result of the Government's educational programme and which I have had the privilege of leading in that regard:

- The government programme of investment in information and communications technology for the education system, together with related professional development of teachers, representing a key strategy for the support of the future learning society.

- The Education Act, 1998, which provides an appropriate and comprehensive legislative underpinning for the education system for the first time since the foundation of the State.

- The responses of the technological sector of higher education and of the further education sector to identified skill shortages in terms of the increased supply of technicians and teleservices personnel.

- The Review of the Points System for entry to higher education which has the objective of further streamlining access and increasing participation in the future.

- The Qualifications (Education and Training) Act, 1999 and its implications for the quality, relevance and co-ordination of developments and certification in further, higher technological, adult and continuing education and training. The Act enjoys the positive support of the seven existing universities and will supplement certification achievements resulting from second-level education.

- The Green Paper on Adult Education and the imminent White Paper which will focus on addressing the specific and general deficits and needs of our adult population, in particular for adults who did not get the opportunity or who otherwise did not benefit from the strengths of our education system at the initial attempt.

The Learning Society and Learning Organisations

In supporting the implementation of these and other milestones, the Department of Education and Science, in concert with other organisations, must proactively set its face at becoming a true learning organisation of the future. Learning organisations are the essence of the learning society. In 1990, Peter M. Senge highlighted the importance of creating learning organisations for the attention of the world in his book, *The Fifth Discipline: The Art and Practice of the Learning Organisation*. Based at the Massachusetts Institute of Technology and the elected chairman of the governing council of the Society for Organisational Learning, Senge popularised systems thinking and focused the spotlight on learning in the workplace as never before. In so doing, he gained the attention of the business world and rallied executives, managers, researchers, consultants and performance improvement practitioners to rethink the basic concepts of leadership and learning.

As a society, we must begin to recognise and appreciate that today's challenges of instant change, rapid ageing of information and higher demand for innovation require organisations that learn – not only to solve problems but to build the capacity to avoid creating problems. The reality is that these challenges require organisations to radically transform themselves, and the critical shift is from organising for control to organising for learning.

Work on the art and practice of the learning organisation has achieved the broad acceptance that learning cannot exist apart from action and must become a way of life rather than a series of episodic events. In this sense, learning is not simply about teaching or about taking in new information or about new ideas; it is about enhancing the capacity for effective action.

New Approaches to Facilitating Access and the Achievement of Competence

A key element of the provision of more and better education for everybody is how we can facilitate people to measure their own improvement and progress. Finding the answer to this question is essential in terms of providing for people who learn in different ways, at different times and at different rates. New approaches to assessing achievement and the nature of competence are therefore required for the emerging learning society. Robert Glaser (National Centre for Research on Evaluation, Standards and Student Testing, University of Pittsburgh) who coined the term *criterion referenced measurement* more than thirty years ago, has postulated (1997) the need for greater attention and new approaches to testing and assessment relating to:

- Facilitating access to education, and

- The achievement of competence.

Glaser's work is critical of the way that testing and assessment have become institutionalised in education systems, maintaining that current practices are based on misconceptions from the past with inevitable and consequent undesirable results.

Specifically, with regard to access to education, Glaser's criticism concerns the fact that testing and assessment have been historically related to differentiating individuals only on the basis of a single measure of intelligence. He recommends new approaches aimed at:

- The identification of prior knowledge (or the foundations of ability and competence)

- Utilising different intelligences that can be brought to individual learning, and

- Enabling self-regulatory abilities such as task performance, problem-solving and situational analysis/comprehension.

In terms of the achievement of competence, Glaser argues that the practices in use today are based on an implicit behavioural psychology, conceived in the past, which cannot adequately describe the complex processes of thinking, reasoning and problem-solving in ways that are now possible and necessary. He calls for the use of more coherent structures of information and the nature of organised knowledge to drive modern techniques of assessing achievement and competence. In addition, he urges further research on these matters and on the use of testing and learning as an interactive endeavour.

It is imperative that we begin to take account of such critical issues as these in the context of providing more relevant education and training for all in the future, and most particularly in keeping learners centre stage with as much control as possible over their own learning, integrated with assessment.

Conclusion

Although our education system is held in high esteem at home and abroad, and we are making significant improvements and progress in responding to change, much more needs to be done. It will require everybody, individuals and organisations, working together to make the transition to a learning society. It will also require more systematic account to be taken of developments and research, such as the examples I have mentioned, if we are to move forward on the basis of the most up to date knowledge and expertise available. It is only through the synergistic effects of working collaboratively and systemically that we will not merely survive the technological revolution but succeed in harnessing its potential towards achieving the benefits of the learning society for all of our people.

Michael Enright's record in teaching, public life and public service indicates that he had an abiding interest in the issues that are characteristic of the emerging learning society. He was in the process of making his own particular contribution to the work of TEASTAS and ultimately to the Qualifications (Education and Training) Act, 1999 when his life was so tragically cut short. I believe he would have approved of the progress we have made and will undoubtedly continue to make in the foreseeable future.

In Memory of Michael Enright
(1952–1997)

I first met Michael Enright at a Wexford Trades Council meeting when he was chairman of that body. We met from time to time after that, usually at some meeting connected with my union, the AEEU, or with the Trades Council. As a committed trade unionist myself, I soon found that I shared many of Mick's ideas on the importance of the union movement to improve the conditions of workers.

The event that certainly made a major impression on me was the publication of Michael Enright's *Men of Iron* (Wexford Council of Trade Unions, 1987) which has become a classic in trade union history in Wexford. This history of the epic struggle between the foundry workers and their employers filled a large gap in the story of Irish trade unionism because so little had been written about the lockouts in Wexford. In fact, as Peter Cassells commented in his foreword to *Men of Iron*, Irish people could "be forgiven for deducing that the entire history of Irish trade unionism took place within a five-mile radius of O'Connell Bridge". We in Wexford owe a debt to Michael who took the time and trouble to research and record the history of the period. I also had a personal reason for an interest in this struggle, due to the fact that one uncle and both of my grandfathers were employed in Pierce's and the Star ironworks in Wexford.

It was later that I began to notice Michael as a politician, and I probably wouldn't have become involved in politics only for Mick. Although I had a deep interest in left-wing politics, it was purely as a spectator because, as we all know, politics is a great blood sport — much safer to view from the sidelines! My interest would have stayed that way except for Michael; his ability to persuade and motivate is renowned. I think I can speak for most of those who were in Democratic Left in Wexford that they wouldn't have joined the party but for Michael's powers of persuasion.

In this brief tribute I can barely touch on Michael's achievements in local government, and in politics in general. I recall the part he played in the anti-nuclear protests in Carnsore. This has become one of the greatest examples of how "people power", when properly marshalled, can make large and very powerful interests reverse their decisions. Thanks to many like Michael who took part in this campaign, Wexford (and indeed Ireland) is nuclear-free today.

There was, of course, Michael's fight to win compensation for the many old people and unemployed to buy cookers when the Gas Company suddenly closed. And he was a leader of the successful campaigns to abolish water charges and to win equality in arrears for women discriminated against in the social welfare code. Also, he was instrumental in establishing the Centres for the Unemployed in Wexford and New Ross. As a teacher, Michael's interest in education and sport, as two of the better ways to help in the development of young people, shone out.

Michael was elected to Wexford Corporation in 1985 and 1991 as a Workers' Party candidate, and easily retained his seat for Democratic Left in 1994. In total he contested three Corporation elections, two County Council, four general elections and a European election. In his last general election outing in 1997 he doubled his vote.

Tragically, Michael didn't live to reach his full potential. Thankfully his work was recognised when he was appointed to TEASTAS, the National Certification Body. But the highlight of his political career must surely have been his appointment to the Senate as a Taoiseach's nominee.

No account, however brief, could be complete without mentioning Michael the family man, his devotion to Mary and his daughters Keira and Karla and the importance home played in his life. While many Irishmen go to the pub to unwind after a day's work, I know that Mick preferred to spend any spare time he had, in a very busy life, with his family. Michael was essentially a man with a great love of life and, like many such people, he had a great sense of humour. I travelled to DL meetings in Dublin with him on many Saturdays in the last few years of his life, and on the way back he would often buy a bottle of wine to drink at home that night. I would often chide him for "drinking at home".

On the many election canvasses and campaigns we in his party branch undertook, Mick's sense of fun kept us going. I think that one has to have a sense of humour to stay involved in politics at the grass roots level, especially left-wing politics in Ireland! During the 1997 general election we were canvassing in Kilmore Quay (a small fishing village in south Wexford) and had travelled there in two cars. Mick had the leaflets in the boot of his car. When he opened the boot, we discovered a large box containing what looked like thousands of leaflets especially printed for Kilmore Quay. We asked Mick was it he or head office thought Kilmore Quay was a metropolis? Michael was the eternal optimist!

Michael's untimely death in October 1997 left us all shocked and devastated. His political colleagues in Wexford and New Ross were overcome with grief, but I think the vision that Michael had shared with us all made us more determined to carry on, to keep alive the dream that he had worked for over many years. It has been a great honour to be asked to say a little about my late friend Michael Enright; nobody deserves higher tribute.

Councillor Davy Hynes

✖✖✖✖✖✖

Brecht's lines from the Threepenny Opera, "consider the darkness and the great cold in this vale which resounds with misery", embody how family and friends felt as they stood in Killinick cemetery in County Wexford while Michael Enright was buried in bright October sunshine, aged forty-five. Earlier as we walked down Bride Street, I overheard a man telling another how Michael had helped him join Alcoholics Anonymous; a woman said simply "Michael was a great help to me". These were the people to whom he had devoted his life as a political organiser, as a councillor for the Workers' Party and following its establishment, Democratic Left. As chairperson of Wexford Trades Council he came to know the working class in a town of declining metallurgical industries, with a silted port and new half-finished housing estates where welfare often predominated over work. *Men of Iron*, his history of the Wexford lockout dealt with the radical impetus which grew out of the town's foundries; his work as a councillor involved an unsentimental engagement with what that world had become.

Michael's political evolution may have appeared erratic — the U.C.G. Labour Party, the Socialist Labour Party, the Workers' Party and finally, Democratic Left. But this variety of memberships was all of a piece, consistent with his relentless exploration of socialism as an evolving methodology of liberation rather than a rigid doctrine of neo-theological certainties. Michael was always both teacher and student — even his honeymoon was intensely political. He and Mary began their wonderful marriage in the Soviet Union, then seldom visited from Ireland and often, for the Left, a mythologised Otherworld. The reality of the Soviet achievement was one of the topics which most exercised him as he and I travelled to work together for a number of years and he brought an extraordinary intellectual restlessness to this and to the many other issues we debated.

Irish nationalism and the rights of Ulster Protestantism were interrogated by him at similar depth as he evolved a position on the varieties of Irish identity which only achieved its full political articulation with the establishment of Democratic Left.

As is the socialist tradition, his conclusions issued in practical political action: the fierce independence he brought to Wexford Corporation and to the Trades Council, his work for Chilean political refugees, his establishment of the Centres for the Unemployed at New Ross and Wexford, his membership of the Teacher's Union of Ireland, his participation in the Peace Train and, latterly, his membership of the Seanad and of the board of Teastas, the state agency for third-level certification outside the universities.

Proinsias De Rossa's oration at Killinick, with its perfectly chosen quotation from Raymond Carver, helped fortify us all in the face of tragedy from which little solace can be drawn. To Mary, whom he met in UCG — Michael from Ennis, Mary from Moycullen — and his adored daughters Karla and Keira, we can only offer as consolation his life's work with its affirmation that the public space, the political, is the primary determinant in all our lives.

Proinsias O'Drisceoil